PRAISE FOR *MY N...*

"*My Neighbor, My Self* is a gift to those of us
wanting to live out Jesus's greatest commandment:
to love God, neighbor, and self. This fascinating read
draws on Scripture and engaging stories to illustrate
how these three loves interrelate and reinforce each
other. Chase anticipates challenges we may face and
transparently shares successes and failures in a way
both inspiring and practical. Questions at the end
of each chapter promote meaningful reflection for
individuals or groups."

—PAUL V. SORRENTINO

Director of Religious & Spiritual Life Emeritus, Amherst College

"Chase writes with moving vulnerability about her
personal experiences getting to know, love, and
help the homeless, and of how these friendships
deepened her relationship with Jesus. Sharing her
own joys, sorrows, and challenges, she also high-
lights surprising gifts others have discovered while
practicing 'neighbor love.' Here are reflective insights
and useful tips for any reader seeking to travel his or
her own 'Matthew 25 journey.'"

—ALAN R. BURT

author of *Blessings of the Burden: Reflections
and Lessons in Helping the Homeless*

"Storytelling and insightful inspiration reminiscent of Henri Nouwen—that's what I see in *My Neighbor, My Self.* Elise Chase gently leads us on a spiritual journey—her own, her community's—that illustrates how inner growth is both a cause and effect of Samaritan-style concern for neighbors. The empowering love of Jesus is the key. Elise's book is a guidepost."

—EVELYN BENCE

author of *Room at My Table: Preparing Heart and Home for Christian Hospitality* and *Mary's Journal*

"With courage and vulnerability, Chase invites us to plumb the depths of community, friendship, and service, and reminds us that God's love is made complete in *us.* Chase reminds me that I have a soul, and that God's perfect love casts out fear. She gives me courage to invite Jesus and others below the surface of my life, and to draw near to people who are in need and in pain. This book is for anyone who wants to move beyond thin community and casual relationships into the depths of knowing and being known."

—BILL HODGEMAN

Senior Pastor, College Church, Northampton, Massachusetts

My Neighbor, My Self

My Neighbor, My Self

Beginning Reflections on a Spirituality of Service

ELISE CHASE

RESOURCE *Publications* · Eugene, Oregon

MY NEIGHBOR, MY SELF
Beginning Reflections on a Spirituality of Service

Resource Publications
An Imprint of Wipf and Stock Publishers
199 W. 8th Ave., Suite 3
Eugene, OR 97401

www.wipfandstock.com

PAPERBACK ISBN: 978-1-6667-3072-2
HARDCOVER ISBN: 978-1-6667-2257-4
EBOOK ISBN: 978-1-6667-2258-1

12/07/21

To the memory of my beloved husband "Chip"—Reverend Charles Henderson III—who lived whole-heartedly into the two great commandments, faithfully serving both God and neighbors as Priest to Emmanuel Episcopal Church in Adams, New York, and Zion Episcopal Church in Pierrepont Manor, New York,

and

to the memory of "Pastor Dave"—Reverend David Paul McDowell—beloved pastor of College Church in Northampton, Massachusetts, for twenty-five years, where he inspired, led, and companioned us in our church's "cot program," an emergency overnight shelter for the homeless.

Contents

Preface

Some books have a long gestation period. This is one of them.

I first began to think about writing *My Neighbor, My Self* during long winter nights while volunteering at an emergency shelter for homeless men and women that a group of us had set up behind the sanctuary at College Church in Northampton, Massachusetts. After supper we would all gather around card tables, guests and volunteers alike, chatting about everything under the sun, sometimes till nearly midnight. Later, lying on one of the rickety canvas cots the Red Cross had loaned to us, I had plenty of time to turn these conversations over and over in my mind and to imagine the book I might someday want to write about it all.

We had started our "cot program" just over three decades ago, to accommodate the overflow of guests that Jessie's House, Northampton's family shelter, had to turn away each evening for lack of space. As it turned out, getting to know these homeless folks who came through our doors was life changing for me. Partly, of course, this was because listening to their stories dramatically expanded my horizons and exploded my limited perspective on the world. But it was more personal than just this. Recently divorced at the time and still struggling with the pain that loss of a marriage can bring, I found that these conversations we were sharing, and the deeper connections with God that we were discovering, were profoundly healing.

As time went on, random thoughts that had been floating through my mind increasingly began to take shape, converging around implications of the second great commandment, "Love your neighbor as yourself" (Luke 10:27). Bit by bit I began drafting up a few ideas—first in my imagination and later, on paper— and blocking out the structure of a potential book.

Life can derail our plans, though, and that is what happened to me. Just as I was completing a very rough draft several years later and starting to put out feelers to a couple of potential publishers, my mother fell ill down in New Jersey. She fought a protracted battle with cancer and following her death my father's health failed as well. For close to a decade, I juggled job responsibilities with family challenges, often commuting over two hundred miles each way on long weekends to tend to my parents' needs. Finally, when my father's illness reached crisis proportions, I brought him up to Northampton, where he remained until his death. Needless to say, long before this I had totally forgotten about the book I had once been working on. Demands of parent care had completely driven it from my mind.

After my dad's death I might have considered returning to the project, but instead, after early retirement from my job as a reference librarian, I found myself becoming unexpectedly involved in a new friendship with an Episcopal priest who lived near Syracuse, New York. Over the course of the next year as we became closer (and I put a lot more mileage on my car!), my life took another significant new turn. We married early in 2010, I relocated to New York, and for a couple of years until my husband Chip's retirement at the end of 2011, the thought of writing this book remained the farthest thing from my mind. I did have the opportunity to grow more deeply into its themes, though. I was living with them rather than putting them down on paper.

Chip was a "twenty-four seven" kind of priest, and we became a real ministry team together as I joined various groups in his church and got increasingly involved in the loving and close fellowship of believers in his congregation. Sometimes I was the "stay-at-home" one, of course, like the night when the phone rang at two o'clock in the morning and one of Chip's parishioners begged him to come over to the house then and there, as she feared her terminally ill son might not last till the next day. Chip's initial impulse was to go first thing in the morning; a "lake effect" blizzard was raging that night, and this family lived a half hour from the rectory, over dangerously rutted roads. Chip couldn't sleep, though, as he lay there thinking about it all. So of course, he got in the car half an hour later and made that dangerous drive. I finally saw him again about four-thirty in the morning. "Love your neighbor as yourself," indeed! As I said, being Chip's wife in that church community was truly to be living with this theme.

When Chip retired at the end of 2011 we returned to Northampton to my little ranch house, and immersion in our marriage continued to take center stage for me. We thought of ourselves as "bridge people," longing to facilitate better understanding between different church communities, and together we were involved both at College Church and at St. John's, Northampton's Episcopal church, heading over each Sunday after St. John's eight o'clock service to attend College Church's ten o'clock one. We joined groups in both churches as well, so that sometimes (rightly or wrongly!) Chip claimed he was busier in retirement than he had been before. I sold my tiny vacation home on Cape Cod so we could buy a little condo in beautiful Rockport on Cape Ann, north of Boston, where Chip's first wife had given birth to their two children and where Chip had other longstanding family roots. That condo was an extraordinary blessing for us; it provided a place where we could both find much needed rest, and Chip spent a lot of time there painting local scenes he had loved since he was a young man.

It was a great shock when Chip unexpectedly passed away in December of 2019. Nor was that the only shock, for a couple of months later the pandemic hit, and COVID-19 took over all of our lives.

With the cancellation of normal outside activities and the resulting weeks and months alone here in my Northampton house for nearly a year and a half, I have had plenty of time to think . . . and think . . . and think. One of the things I found myself thinking about, not surprisingly, was the writing I had begun so many years earlier. One day I picked it up again, began to look it over, and asked myself whether possibly I could do something with it now. The book you are holding is the answer to that question.

My biggest concern was whether to include more recent personal material in the narrative, drawn from my years of parent care and remarriage, and thus to bring my own story in *My Neighbor, My Self* explicitly up to date, as it were. It goes without saying that there is much I could share from those years that would be highly relevant to the theme of loving our neighbors. The more I thought about it, though, the more I realized that doing this would almost surely mean writing an entirely new book. It would mean adding so much different material that it would change the organic structure of the whole and would force me to eliminate a lot of what I already had.

I didn't want to do that; I cared too much about the individuals and experiences in the manuscript as it stood. So, except for adding a number of new illustrative stories drawn from other people's lives, revising many of the more theoretical sections, and, of course, editing the overall manuscript, I decided to leave the shape of the narrative as it was. What I have done, though, is to write a brief Concluding Word in which I share a bit about how caring for my parents and marrying Chip helped me to gain a deeper understanding and appreciation of the book's main themes. God has changed me enough through these experiences that I have definitely brought new spiritual insights to the task of revising the manuscript. In that sense, the whole text of *My Neighbor, My Self* does indeed reflect what God has been showing me during this time.

As I say so often throughout this book, we can all grow into the people God wants us to become as we live into caring relationships with our neighbors. In this sense we all have an ongoing opportunity to find a deeper identity in the Lord, to become richer women and men through relationships with others, and to discover both new reasons and new ways to surrender more fully to God. Indeed, our individual journeys as we seek to love our neighbors as ourselves can enrich us until the day we die.

Acknowledgments

So many people have played a part in birthing this book that it would be impossible to mention them all. First and foremost are the guests and volunteers whom I came to know while working with our emergency cot program to shelter homeless men and women at College Church in Northampton, Massachusetts. Experiences we shared together entered so deeply into my soul that it is impossible even to imagine who I might be today without them, and I am more grateful than I can express for the gift of these relationships. In particular, the vision, guidance, and godly presence of our late pastor, David P. McDowell, meant so much to us all. In acknowledging the blessings of getting to know the folks who were guests in our shelter, by the way, I just want to mention that in all cases I have changed their names.

Friends from College Church, St. John's Episcopal Church, and elsewhere who have graciously shared their stories with me for inclusion in this book have also played an essential role, and I am most thankful to them. I want to mention Eartha Harris and Judy Donovan McCurdy by name, as they have been so deeply inspiring to me. Thank you, Eartha and Judy.

When I was working on a first draft of this book a number of years ago, several friends helped by reading the manuscript as it stood at that time and offering suggestions. For this I particularly want to thank Andrea Bundy and Barbara Gawle. I also want to thank Linda McCullough Moore and Cynthia Weinrich for recent stimulating and wonderfully helpful conversations.

Finally, when it came to the challenge of formatting the Word document to meet publication requirements, I want to thank Cathie McCoy and Mary Riso for their cheerful and invaluable help. My gratitude to both of you, Cathie and Mary, is boundless. I couldn't have done it without you! And last, but most definitely not least, I am more grateful than I can possibly express in words to Linda Knaack, who so kindly let me use her computer when my own suddenly died just as I was trying to finish this project.

Introduction

One Sunday morning at College Church in Northampton, Massachusetts, when we were setting up our emergency shelter for the homeless, Pastor Tim Christenson was preaching a sermon on Jesus' words in Matthew 22:37–39: "'Love the Lord your God with all your heart and with all your soul and with all your mind.' This is the first and greatest commandment. And the second is like it: 'Love your neighbor as yourself.'"

Loving God fully involves a multi-faceted response, Pastor Christenson was explaining. God calls forth our fear and reverence, our loyalty, trust, and awe; God invites us to give him thanks and praise; God inspires us to offer him service, repentance, and passion; and much, much more.

Unexpectedly, a chuckle from the pulpit caught me off guard. "Now, most folks I know—myself included—seem able to sustain a perfect love of God, as a general rule, for about two nanoseconds." The congregation laughed appreciatively. And then Pastor Tim added something that really caught my attention. "That's why we need the reality check of the second great commandment. If we leave church meditating on our love for God, and someone interrupts our thoughts to ask for a ride home, our response to that interruption is a pretty good indication of how deep our love really goes."

Oh! I drew in my breath with excitement. For one of the most striking lessons I was discovering right at that time in my own spiritual journey was how closely the great commandments are actually interrelated. Yes, the second is a reality check on our obedience to the first, but it can be even more than this. In fact, it can be a wonderful resource for learning to love the Lord more deeply. Seeking to follow God's call to love our neighbors as ourselves, we can be drawn into transformative relationships and blessed in surprising ways by finding new intimacy with him.

HOW LOVING OUR NEIGHBORS CAN HELP US LOVE GOD

I've come to appreciate this link between the two great commandments more and more over the years. By way of explanation, let me share a portion of my story.

I came to faith initially at a time of great personal need when I faced the anguish of unwanted divorce. In that crisis, I—an agnostic—was surprised to find myself crying out to Jesus. In return, I was blessed by an extraordinary sense of his presence and love. Instinctively I clung to him as to a lifeline, while my marriage and my former sense of identity disintegrated around me. Later, building a new "single-again" life, I continued to cling to Jesus, seeking—and receiving—both guidance and grace to meet the many challenges confronting me.

Yet gradually, as my immediate problems began to be solved and new natural resources of job, home, and friends began to fall into place, something subtle and insidious was happening. Almost without realizing it, I was beginning to depend more on these things than on the One who had met me at the point of the original crisis. At last, I had to admit that my initial response to the Lord had been far from the kind of committed love he desires from us and the kind that he deserves.

To love God fully is to be so captivated by his triune mystery and beauty that we long to give ourselves entirely to him: God the Father, perfect in justice and mercy, in sovereignty and grace; God the Son, pouring out love as he hands himself over to death on the cross for our redemption; God the Holy Spirit, empowering and gifting believers to begin living out here on earth their unfolding roles in the kingdom that is to come. To love God completely is to be so trusting of God's purposes, so grateful for all that he is and has been to us in our lives, that we are willing to say with Christ, "Yet not as I will, but as you will" (Matthew 26:39).

Clearly, my own love had been quite different from this. It had been what C. S. Lewis calls "Need-love" in his Introduction to *The Four Loves*.[1] This condition of utter dependence on God is our necessary starting place and surely remains foundational in our relationship with the Lord, but if we want to move into deeper faith, we need to learn other ways of loving God as well. We must be willing to take the risks involved in honestly seeking God's will for our lives; we must become ready to abandon the natural "security props" on which we have depended, so as to step out into the new places to which God calls us. We can only do this as the Holy Spirit enables us to trust that any new life into which the Lord invites us will be infinitely richer than the life we live now, surrounded by our accustomed comforts. For my own part, I was often confounded by the many questions this challenge posed. What might God ask of me? What sacrifices might I be required to make? Where might I find myself transplanted?

Yet in the midst of the uncertainty, it was as if God kept calling me back to Jesus' words in Matthew 22:37–39: "'Love the Lord your God with all your heart and with all your soul and with all your mind.' This is the first and greatest commandment. And the second is like it: 'Love your neighbor as yourself.'" That second commandment in particular was highlighted in my heart, as if it contained an answer to my dilemma.

Could it be, I found myself wondering, that experiences which come to us as we reach out compassionately to others can help us to bridge the gap between a self-centered response to God and the self-risking love to which God calls us? Could it be that as we practice shifting our focus from our own needs to the needs of the people around us, the Holy Spirit will work in our hearts and deepen our capacity to love and trust the Lord? These thoughts came to me more and more often, until I realized I had better pay attention and begin to put them into practice. So before very long, I

1. Lewis, *Four Loves*, 11

found myself volunteering at a local homeless shelter. One thing led to another, and next thing I knew, I was helping our interdenominational church set up an emergency cot program to help with the shelter's overflow during cold winter nights.

Thus, began a remarkable new stage in my life. It was quite striking how, as I became more immersed in working with homeless people, I began to experience real breakthroughs in my own relationship with God. Distractions and anxieties that often plagued my prayers at other times were somehow graciously lifted when I was at our shelter, so that I felt close to Jesus in a new way during those hours.

It was like a variation on the theme of the Incarnation. Just as God came to us once in Jesus, so that we could see him, touch him, and respond to him more fully from our limited flesh-and-blood perspective, so now it was if Jesus was coming to us all again—and again, and again—in the needy people we were meeting. For me it was a living encounter with Jesus' words in Matthew 25:40: "I tell you the truth, whatever you did for one of the least of these brothers of mine, you did for me."

WHO THIS BOOK IS FOR

Do you ever long for a closer and more dynamic relationship with God, but feel frustrated, disappointed, and perhaps even lonely because of what seems like a lack of intimacy in your prayer life? Similarly, do you ever find yourself wishing for deeper spiritual connections with others in your church family and in your wider community? Jesus prayed that God's kingdom might come on earth as it is in heaven. Do you ever wonder what this might really mean, and what it might feel like to catch glimpses of God's embryonic kingdom in your "real life" fellowship of believers? If so, then I encourage you to reflect imaginatively on some of the ideas and stories contained in these pages and to share with God any thoughts that come to you as you do.

As the subtitle indicates, this book offers *beginning* reflections on a spirituality of service. Often when we first start to explore

God's call into neighbor-love, we can feel insecure or overwhelmed. Perhaps we are so conscious of all the pain in the world, and all the troubles of the immediate folks we are trying to help, that we cannot believe our paltry efforts could really make a difference. Perhaps we doubt that our prayers could ever be powerful enough to touch the enormity of the problems. Or we may look around at people who are living lives of radical service and—comparing ourselves with them—feel discouraged at the outset, convinced that we could never reach that kind of spiritual maturity.

Each person's journey is unique, though. God welcomes and meets us all wherever we happen to find ourselves and will guide us on from there, one step at a time. So, this book is for people who feel nudged to seek a deeper and more fruitful relationship with the Lord, with their fellow believers, and with their neighbors, even as they struggle with possible resistance, self-doubt, or ambivalence that may be standing in the way.

For people like this and for those accompanying them— friends, family members, pastors—I have one central message. In the command to love our neighbors as ourselves, I am convinced that God has given us a profound resource for our journey into faith. If we can help each other begin to tap into this resource in all its dimensions, we will discover a deeper relationship with the Lord, with one another, and with ourselves.

It really is a paradox. In an important sense, the first great commandment—to love the Lord with all our heart, soul, strength, and mind—is obviously primary and foundational since our connection with God ideally inspires us to reach out to our neighbors and keeps us grounded for guidance and inspiration as we do. We cannot really love others fully and fruitfully unless God loves them *through* us. Yet even if we do not yet experience such a deep connection with the Lord, our beginning efforts at neighbor-love can still help us start to move forward. Graciously, our very inadequacy reminds us of our dependence on God and calls us to prayer. Then, as we turn to God, sharing our relational failures with him, we may find that those very failures become raw material for his healing work in our lives.

Tom Berlin makes just this point in *Reckless Love: Jesus' Call to Love Our Neighbor,* noting that nothing reveals what he calls "barnacles on the soul" more dramatically than sincere attempts to obey the second great commandment. Once we commit to this effort, he tells us, it won't be long before we see ourselves more clearly and come to realize how much we need God's help if we are to grow beyond sinful habits and attitudes that are holding us back from loving others as God wants us to do.[2] When we experience the Lord's guidance and love for us in the midst of our imperfections, our love for him deepens, according to the principle set forth in 1 John 4:19: "We love because he first loved us." As this happens, we also discover a more biblical self-love, the kind to which Jesus implicitly invites us in his command that we love our neighbors "as ourselves."

HOW THIS BOOK IS ORGANIZED

This core theme—that we can find deeper union with God and discover our true selves in the Lord as we seek to love our neighbors under his guidance—shapes the structure of *My Neighbor, My Self.*

Part One, "My Neighbor," shares basic guidelines and illustrative examples regarding steps people can prayerfully take on the practical human level to become more fruitfully involved in helping others, either individually or in groups. Chapters 1, 2, and 3 explore a number of issues: working through our initial resistance to center anew in Jesus; connecting with the inner resources of our own pain and joy, the special gifts we have to offer, our emerging sense of call; and finally, coming together for support and prayer with a group of others who share common concerns and with whom we can pray as we begin to experience the corporate reality of God's unfolding kingdom.

Moving beyond the guidelines in Part One, Part Two, "My Self," looks in more depth at the transformation that can occur in our hearts when the Holy Spirit meets us in our flawed attempts to serve. One question undergirds all the reflections here: What is biblical self-love really all about, and how can it be nurtured?

2. Berlin, *Reckless Love,* 21–24.

Chapters 4, 5, and 6 suggest that we can begin to find an answer to this question as we reach out to our neighbors. Experiences then come to us which open our hearts and make us more receptive to the Lord's work in our lives. As this happens, we find ourselves better able to discern our authentic identity in God, to discover the Lord's transforming power in our relationships, and, finally, to find fulfillment in greater intimacy with him. Thus, we grow into our *true selves*; we reach bedrock knowledge of who we really are and what gives our lives meaning and purpose; we experience biblical self-love in the way that God surely intends.

This perspective explains why one question friends have posed about the book's format strikes me as central. The question is this: Why does the section "My Neighbor" precede the section "My Self"? Shouldn't it be the other way around? Is it really possible to love others in a healthy way if we haven't learned to love ourselves?

In an important sense, the answer is *no*, of course not. If we cannot give and receive forgiveness in our personal lives, we will probably find it hard to facilitate reconciliation in the lives of others. If we are judgmental toward ourselves and have little self-acceptance, we may have trouble conveying acceptance to those around us. Some folks do need to work prayerfully with their own struggles, and perhaps to seek help in doing so before they focus on neighbor-love.

It is especially true that those who are prone to codependent patterns, seeking to shore up their identities by attaching themselves to others, or to flee their own responsibilities by "serving" the folks around them, need to begin concentrating on their own issues and concerns if they hope to discover new growth and to be there for others in healthy ways. Chapter 5 touches on this subject under the topic "Loving Others, Self-Love, and Codependency."

Yet it is also true that ultimately, we cannot discover who we really are in God, or the contributions we are called to make to the Lord's unfolding kingdom, unless we are moved by concern for other people. It is as if our caring calls forth the *true self* that needs affirming, in contrast to the *false self* we are called to relinquish. In this sense, biblical self-love often deepens through our relationships with the neighbors God places on our hearts. So, I have chosen to discuss pathways and perspectives that encourage neighbor-love first, in Part One, before turning to examine our new love of self in the Lord which Part Two explores. It is certainly possible, though, for readers to read these two sections in reverse order if they prefer.

An additional question may arise for some. If love for God is our ultimate goal, and God's love for us is our foundational resource, shouldn't the book have a separate section devoted to our relationship with the Lord?

In fact, an early draft of the manuscript did contain such a section. But it became clear to me as I read it all over that this was not the best way to proceed. So many people have written more eloquently than I ever could on the awesome character of our God, or on spiritual disciplines for moving from the head to the heart as we learn to love God more fully. I think (almost at random!) of the profound reflections on God's attributes contained in *The Knowledge of the Holy* by A.W. Tozer and, when it comes to discussing spiritual disciplines, of *Spiritual Formation: Following the Movements of the Spirit,* a rich and profound posthumous integration of many of Henri Nouwen's published and unpublished writings on this subject. Books like these are wonderful resources to deepen our love for the Lord and enrich our prayer lives. But where are the books to help people grow closer to God through the relational experience of neighbor-love? They are much harder to find.

Several recent and wonderful examples do exist, to be sure. One is Tom Berlin's *Reckless Love,* which I mentioned earlier. Another is Alan R. Burt's *Blessings of the Burden: Reflections and Lessons in Helping the Homeless,* in which Burt shares his own advocacy journey with moving vulnerability, always conscious of Jesus' call to care for "the least of these." Then there is Mark Labberton's *The Dangerous Act of Loving Your Neighbor: Seeing Others Through the Eyes of Jesus.* This remarkable and provocative book considers the second great commandment against the backdrop of a world submerged in suffering and injustice, suggesting that our great spiritual task is to open ourselves to God so that God can transform our ordinary, often indifferent hearts into hearts more ready to respond to the pain we see all around us. To read this book is to embark on a profound spiritual journey into deeper love of God and neighbor.

For the most part, though, many of the newer books on neighbor-love, probably not surprisingly, have tended to focus more on practical tips and techniques for striking up potential helping (or witnessing?) relationships—sometimes in highly creative and catchy ways, as in Patrick Linnell's *Grace Bomb: The Surprising Impact of Loving Your Neighbors*. Titles like this certainly have an important role to play. But save for occasional words of encouragement about how to grow through God's guidance when outreach attempts backfire, they do not generally focus on our own inner growth as we seek to live more deeply into neighbor-love—the theme that I am emphasizing here.

One author whose wise, reflective writing gained a lot of attention a few decades ago, and who beautifully explored the relationship between outer acts of service and inner transformation, was the late Elizabeth O 'Connor. Her remarkable books about the ecumenical Church of the Saviour in Washington, DC, have been such a rich resource and influence for me in my own life that it is impossible for me to imagine the course that my journey would have taken were it not for her work. Without question, O'Connor's vision has played a huge role in helping to shape the structure of this present book.

Because *My Neighbor, My Self* explores the growth and healing we can discover through relationships—with God, with our neighbors, and with ourselves—it seemed important that the narrative be experiential as well as theoretical, to help readers respond with their hearts as well as with their minds. For this reason, I have shared some stories springing from my own involvement with homeless men and women, as well as illustrative examples from the lives of friends and others engaged in various forms of service or lay ministry. Hopefully, this will give body to the ideas being explored and will help people identify imaginatively as they read. Finally, each chapter concludes with reflective questions to personalize the issues raised and to help readers—alone or in groups—apply the principles to their own lives.

The writing itself has been an extraordinary journey, for time and again as I was working on the manuscript, it seemed that God brought to my attention just the right people and experiences to illustrate on the level of the heart insights I had been struggling to express with intellectual understanding alone. In this respect, the birthing of this book has felt like one long unfolding prayer: a prayer that has been graciously answered.

PART ONE

My Neighbor

Chapter 1

Who Is My Neighbor?

One night many years ago I was feeling crushed by personal concerns as I struggled to build a new life after unwanted divorce. Early the next morning, I awoke in the predawn hours to a startling experience.

As I lay there half-conscious in my little bedroom, dimly in my mind's eye I found myself envisioning Jesus. He was standing in a wide, dark field that was littered with bodies: starving, broken bodies of women, men, and children. He was walking straight out into the midst of them, but then he paused a moment, turned toward me, and held out his hand as if to invite me along. Would I come? Finally, as I stood on the sidelines paralyzed, unable to follow, he turned away again, walked on ahead, and disappeared into the darkness.

Transfixed, I lay there. It was not that I took my dream vision to be a supernatural encounter with the Lord, necessarily. Our imaginations can take us to strange places in the wee hours of the morning. Still, it was profoundly disturbing.

Jesus' apparent invitation froze me, for it seemed to contain implications for my relationship with God that were frightening to contemplate and that nudged me to reflect on issues I might prefer to ignore. At that time I shelved the whole matter; to deal with it then simply felt too overwhelming. Yet on some level, I knew that eventually I would have to face the questions it had raised.

THE CHALLENGE OF THE GOOD SAMARITAN

Those who encounter Jesus' radical presence in the gospel narratives are often similarly defensive. Take, for example, the exchange recorded in Luke 10:25–29.

In this familiar passage, "an expert in the law" wants to test Jesus and asks him what he must do to inherit eternal life. "What is written in the Law?" Jesus asks, and his questioner answers, "'Love the Lord your God with all your heart and with all your soul and with all your strength and with all your mind'; and, 'Love your neighbor as yourself.'" Jesus approves. "Do this," he tells the man, "and you will live."

That legal expert just can't let it be, though. Wanting to "justify" himself (and still, one suspects, wanting to test Jesus), he insists on a narrower, more manageable definition. So he asks, "And who is my neighbor?"

I think I can understand something of that man's motivation, at least when it comes to his personal wish to narrow down the definition of "neighbor." Actually, I suspect most of us can understand, if we stop to think about it. "Who is my neighbor?" Wouldn't we all, deep down, prefer a precise answer to that question, one we can get a handle on so we can keep the matter under manageable control? Don't we instinctively seek to defend ourselves against our half-conscious anxiety that the needs of all the "others" might, if we really faced them, drain us of our own meager resources, or take us into areas of experience that could prove uncomfortable? Surely, we rationalize, by having done this or that particular duty—by having made that casserole for the potluck outreach, or by having visited that woman in the nursing home—we have somehow fulfilled the obligation.

When the expert in the law tries this approach, though, seeking to get a narrower definition to let himself off the hook, his question backfires. Instead of playing into his hands, Jesus tells him a story in Luke 10:30–37 with very disturbing implications.

A man, Jesus begins, was beaten and nearly killed by robbers he met along the road. A priest who happened to witness this passed by on the other side without stopping, as did a Levite. Then, Jesus continues in verses 33–35:

> But a Samaritan, as he traveled, came where the man was; and when he saw him, he took pity on him. He went to him and bandaged his wounds, pouring on oil and wine. Then he put the man on his own donkey, took him to an inn and took care of him. The next day he took out two silver coins and gave them to the innkeeper. 'Look after him,' he said, 'and when I return, I will reimburse you for any extra expense you may have.'

Finally, in verse 36, Jesus concludes with a compelling question. "Which of these three do you think was a neighbor to the man who fell into the hands of robbers?"

How many questions this story must have raised as that expert in the law reflected on it in his mind! And aren't they similar to questions we may find ourselves asking, as Jesus challenges us today?

The priest and the Levite who saw the beaten man merely "happened" to do so. Does this mean that our neighbor is anyone, anyone at all, whose need happens to come to our attention, whose path we unexpectedly cross as we are focusing on our own agendas and responsibilities? Besides, the priest and the Levite were both respectable and respected figures in the religious culture of their day; is no one, then, no matter how dignified their status, exempt from the mandate to respond to sudden intrusions into their lives by anonymous strangers?

The one who did stop to help, moreover, was a religious and cultural outcast according to the standards of the time. The wrong group. The wrong class. The wrong religion. A *Samaritan*. And yet . . . Jesus is praising him! Could it be that the marginal one with no status or socially sanctioned responsibilities (but for that very reason, perhaps, more available to respond with compassion), finds Jesus' favor over and above people who busy themselves with God's "official" work every day of their lives?

It is almost as if Jesus is telling us that regardless of our important duties, we need to remain so humble before him, so open to him and to the people we encounter, that we receive every moment as if from him, always available to take on a new challenge, always seeking his inflowing grace so that we may meet it. Like the Samaritan, Jesus seems to be saying, we need to be willing to be available to the unexpected neighbor, the unexpected need, if that is where he directs us. "Go and do likewise" (Luke 10:37).

Can we actually live this way? Do we really want that degree of openness and vulnerability to Jesus and to all the people around us?

Often, if we are honest, the answer is a clear-cut *no*. We may feel, with some real justification, that we are already overcommitted and overwhelmed. There may be family responsibilities; we may be worn to a frazzle by the demands of work; or possibly we are so submerged in pain over some personal situation that the idea of reaching out to another seems more than we can imagine. Or then again, it may be just the momentary pressures of an unusually hectic day that have temporarily undone us. Whatever the reason, our defenses often go up at the thought of responding openheartedly to the people around us.

For my own part, sometimes I just don't want to think about it all. I don't want to be distracted from my own immediate concerns or to face the mental effort that might be involved. I would so much rather it would all go away. And occasionally I would rather the actual *people* would go away, too—the ones who unexpectedly turn up on any random day. So it was one exhausting morning many years ago that I remember all too well.

I had been on duty at our library's reference desk that particular day. It was lunch hour. I had torn myself away from work (and "torn" is almost literally accurate; it had been a very busy morning!). I was anticipating a few moments in which to wind down over soup and salad before plunging into the activities scheduled for that afternoon.

There had been endless and complicated questions: two out-of-state genealogists wanting to know every leaf and twig on their family trees; a phone call from San Francisco, California, from a historian needing some elusive papers presumably housed somewhere (but where?) in one of our special collections; newspaper reporters from the local paper with immediate deadlines on stories for which they needed hundreds of details confirmed. My head was swimming from it all, and in forty-five minutes I was due for a doctor's appointment (it would take at least fifteen minutes to navigate the crush of noon-hour traffic) before making my way back home to edit a monthly column for *Library Journal* and send it off to New York. Then I had to pack, eat supper, and (by six o'clock) throw my things and myself into the car for a three hour drive to Cape Cod. I needed to be there by nine p.m. on the dot to claim the motel room I had reserved for that night, in preparation for a couple of days' writing in (was this really possible?) a spirit of creative serenity.

Hurrying down the street, reference questions gradually untangling themselves from one another in the cubby-holes of my mind (yes, it was all right; they all really had been taken care of!), I turned into the door of my favorite restaurant, a bookstore cafe with homemade breads and soups and display racks of newspapers and journals. A few moments—glorious thought!—in which to unwind.

And then it happened.

There near the counter—right next to the only empty table in the restaurant, as a matter of fact—sat a woman hunched over her soup that I recognized from the library. I didn't know her name, but I knew her obsession, all right. It was the evils of welfare, and I knew that if I sat at that table next to her, all I would hear about for the next ten minutes would be the welfare system: the ways it was fostering laziness and immorality; the ways it was robbing us of tax dollars; the general catastrophe it was causing. Instinctively, without pause for conscious thought, I whirled around so that my back was to her (had she seen me yet?) and knew that I was going to buy a tuna salad sandwich to go instead of my favorite sausage, kale, and tomato soup to stay.

As I stood there waiting to order, back carefully turned, I heard her begin to speak. "You know what's going on?" she was asking in that rapid, eager voice, every sentence punctuated with the stress of her anxiety, her hunger to be received. "The welfare system is ruining our whole economy. Let me tell you about it . . ."

I waited, wondering what poor stranger she had cornered now, anticipating the hedged, concealed impatience in the voice of her respondent . . . an impatience that certainly would have been in my own voice had I been on the receiving end of that question. But no, I was wrong.

"Gee, that sounds bad. I guess that worries you a lot." The answering voice, a man's, was calm and comfortable, soothing in a neutral, uninvolved sort of way.

"Yes, it's bad, very bad . . ."

"Ummm. Yeah, I can see you feel that way."

The dialogue went on as I put in my order, and then as I paid and collected my sandwich, turning to go, I stole a glance at the owner of this comfortable voice.

It was a youngish man in blue jeans and a rumpled shirt, with curly brown hair and kind, friendly eyes. He stood smiling at my library acquaintance. "Well, gotta go now," he said. He smiled more warmly, put his hand on the woman's shoulder. "You take care, okay?" He clapped her shoulder again, gave her another smile,—right into her eyes, deep, direct, and kind—then ambled off and out of the restaurant.

I looked at my library acquaintance's face. Just for a moment, I could see it clearly: the customary anxiety was there, yes, but there was something else, too. A flicker of something . . . *Wonder*, that was it. Yes, and *gratitude*. And suddenly a huge remorse swept over me for all the times I had so poorly concealed my impatience, especially for this particular time, this particular morning, when I had pretended not to see her.

I tried to make eye contact then, to say hello. But she didn't acknowledge me. It was too late. Her eyes darted away. Once more I tried. "Hi," I said. But my voice was too tentative, too low, and even if she had heard me, I must have sounded terribly awkward. So I gave it up, left the restaurant, and proceeded with my private hectic schedule, my private hectic day.

Love my neighbor as myself? No, many times I am just not very good at it. Not very good at all.

OBEDIENT LISTENING: MARY AND MARTHA

Jesus is asking us to learn to do better. To come into his presence, to open ourselves to his grace, his will, his love. Simply to *be*. Undefended, unguarded, as we relinquish our tight control over our lives.

Can it be by chance that immediately after the parable of the Good Samaritan, Luke gives us the story of Mary and Martha in verses 38–42? Martha welcomes Jesus to her home, where he makes himself comfortable and begins to teach. Martha's sister Mary sits at his feet, drinking in his words, while Martha busies herself with the tasks of being a hostess. "Lord," she complains, "don't you care that my sister has left me to do the work by myself?" But Jesus replies, "Martha, Martha, you are worried and upset about many things, but only one thing is needed. Mary has chosen what is better, and it will not be taken away from her" (Luke 10:40–42).

It is almost as if we have no sooner opened ourselves to the challenge posed by the Good Samaritan story, than Jesus gives us the solution. And what a paradoxical one it is! By placing the story of Mary and Martha immediately after the parable of the Good Samaritan, Luke seems to imply that as we make ourselves available to the needs of those we happen to encounter, we should take our cue from peaceful, contemplative Mary rather than from harried, frenzied Martha. We should be like Martha in the sense of being ready to meet the practical needs, yes; but we should do so in the calm "listening" spirit of Mary, sitting at Jesus' feet.

Could this be possible? True, sometimes I am like Mary. When I have been sick, for example, forced to stay in bed for a couple of days, I have often found myself drawn into deep prayer, "listening" to Jesus with all of my heart. But that is when I am necessarily passive and "useless" for anything else, physically unable to "do" anything. When I am well, though,—most of the time, in fact—often I am a lot more like Martha, as I was that day when I bumped into the woman with the welfare obsession.

What would it be like to carry Mary inside us all the time, as it were—to identify with her in our hearts, even as we are living in the midst of Martha's tasks? What would it mean to be figuratively sitting at Jesus' feet, centered in his presence, listening for his words, in the midst of the hectic bustle of life? Could people really do it? Actually, some people do. I have seen them.

AN EXAMPLE OF CONTEMPLATIVE SERVICE

I think of Judy, a friend in an industrial city in eastern Massachusetts with a long history of involvement in street advocacy. You would never guess from Judy's warm, relaxed presence that her life has been full of such challenging demands.

Talk to Judy a bit and you will learn that as she was raising four boys on her own following divorce and holding down a nine to five nursing job, she was also opening her home on an around-the-clock basis to a variety of people in need.

There was the Cambodian family who had been brought to America by a local organization only to find themselves without enough help. They ended up for a time in Judy's house. "I don't fault these groups," Judy was quick to point out. "They mean well, and they do a lot of good. But sometimes they just don't see all the different aspects of the problem, and how much really needs to be done to get people back on their feet in a new country." Or take the teenage runaway Judy found one day under a picnic table, shivering with pneumonia. He became, for a time, her surrogate son, one of many young people who lived with her and her family off and on over the years.

How did it all happen, how did it unfold? "Look, it's not *me*," she insisted firmly when she first told me about her life. "You've got to know that. Whenever I get to thinking that maybe I'm at the center of this business, everything comes crashing down. It's God working through me, that's all. When you love him totally, then everything just starts to change." She paused and smiled, half to herself. "It's really a love affair, you know. Once a month I go for the weekend to a retreat house by the ocean. Just veg out there by the sea and spend time with Jesus, doing absolutely nothing. We go running down the beach together, he and I. And"—she grinned unexpectedly— "we laugh a lot, too. But you know," and her face sobered, though her eyes were still twinkling, "one thing I've got to say. You better not start saying 'yes' unless you really want your life to be turned upside down. Because it's a very demanding love affair! You better know that right from the start. Once you get into this business of really beginning to love Jesus, you're not going to be the one in control."

OPENING TO GOD'S CALL

Control. That was the operative word.

What was going on that day in the restaurant when I met the "welfare woman"?

Well, I had my agenda. I knew exactly the things that I needed to do, and how much time each would take, and how I needed to move from one task to the next—with dispatch!—if I was going to squeeze it all in. It was completely beyond imagining to me, at that moment, that to open myself to an unwelcome interruption was even a possibility, if my day was not to collapse in smithereens around me. My heart and mind were closed to the notion that God might be able to infuse me with fresh resources, or even that it was an option to ask.

The priest and Levite in the parable of the Good Samaritan—I was behaving exactly like them.

What if I could have been more like Mary that day, as she sat listening to Jesus?

If I had been willing to listen, wouldn't I have realized that a gentle smile, a simple "Hi," when I first saw that woman, wouldn't have robbed me of anything and would, perhaps, even have softened me, made me more easy on myself, helped me to feel more rested and relaxed the rest of that crowded day? Obviously, I wouldn't, indeed *shouldn't*, have dropped all my boundaries and abandoned myself to an open-ended conversation; I could have explained, simply and kindly, that I had a lot of things on my plate and needed to be going. But I didn't have to turn my back and pretend not to see her!

What would that have felt like, if I had been able to say a friendly "hello"?

Why, it would have felt wonderful! A wonderful, relaxing letting go . . .

Oh, to let go of the exhausting effort with which even now I sometimes clutch at control of my endless personal agendas . . . In moments I can almost taste it. It would feel so glorious! So why do I continue to resist? Why do any of us?

No matter how deep and sustained our resistance, though, Jesus continues to invite us into a state of deeper intimacy with him. In refusing explicitly to answer the question, "Who is my neighbor?" and instead reversing it by asking, "Which . . . do you think was a neighbor to the man who fell into the hands of robbers?" Jesus was asking that expert in the law, and surely asks each of us today, to embark on a new journey in search of a deeper identity, a deeper capacity for relationship and love. He can't want us always to be carefully calculating just who our "real" neighbors should be. Surely he wants us instead to be listening every moment for his voice, guidance, and grace.

We may be scared that if we practice living this way Jesus will call us to overwhelming tasks before we are ready. What we need to remember, though, is that Jesus not only loves us, but he knows us better than we know ourselves. Can we dare to trust that if we pay attention to his still small voice, he will point us at exactly the right time toward exactly those people and challenges we are best suited to meet? People and challenges, I mean, that will not only strengthen our identity in the Lord and draw out our authentic self, but also— precisely because of this—nurture our compassion and help us grow closer to God.

Perhaps if we cannot say "yes" to this invitation with complete abandon, we can prayerfully ready ourselves to say an eventual "yes." Can we work with our attitudes and experiences under the Holy Spirit's guidance to begin to cooperate with a call we may not yet totally embrace? Can we take some preliminary steps in learning to *become neighbors* ourselves?

REFLECTIVE QUESTIONS: CHAPTER 1

1. Remember a time when you felt nudged to reach out to an individual or a group in need. How did you learn about this situation? Through a personal conversation? Perhaps from the report of a friend? Through your church, maybe, or through the media? Did you end up getting involved, or did you decide to hold back? How did your response (or lack of response) make you feel?

2. Who are some of the neighbors in your life, literally speaking? How well do you know them? Do you know their names? What do you imagine their image of you might be?

3. If you often feel too pressured to pay attention to others' needs, try taking one week to track the characteristic ways you spend your time. Each evening, jot down the activities in which you engaged, and about how much time you spent on each. Be sure to include the time that you spent in prayer.

4. Reflecting on Luke 10:38–42, with whom do you identify more, Mary or Martha? Why? Can you imagine beginning to integrate a "Mary way of being" into areas of your life where you have "Martha style" responsibilities? Think about some specific ways you would need to change your attitudes and behavior if you were to try and do this.

5. In Luke 18:18–27, where Jesus converses with the rich ruler who feels unable to sell his goods and give to the poor, Jesus notes how hard it is for a rich person to enter God's kingdom. His listeners ask, "Who then can be saved?" Meditate on Jesus' answer, "What is impossible with men is possible with God." What do you think these enigmatic words might mean? Leaving aside for the moment Jesus' call for the rich ruler to sell all his goods, which may have been intended for a specific person at a specific point in time, how might the larger principle behind Jesus' words apply to you in some of your own challenges, when it comes to loving your neighbors?

Chapter 2

Becoming a Neighbor

What would it mean, really, to become a neighbor to the people who cross our paths? How might we find ourselves living if we were more open to Jesus and to others in the way he wants us to be? One way to imagine how it might feel to become a neighbor is to remember a time when someone else was there as a genuine neighbor for *us*.

RECEIVING NEIGHBOR-LOVE FROM ANOTHER

Recently a friend was sharing with a group of us over Zoom how a huge pile of firewood that he had ordered had been dumped next to his house, leaving him overwhelmed at the thought of hauling it up to the woodpile and stacking it in the blazing heat of the day. At that moment a neighbor happened to pass by and, surveying that monumental job and the sweat pouring from his brow, suggested that her son, who was visiting her from California, would be glad to help. At first my friend was reluctant to accept but later changed his mind. When the young man arrived and plunged into the task, it was accomplished so quickly and with such goodwill between the two of them that my friend said it felt like a God given wonder. He ended up doubly grateful— not just for his neighbor's compassion and her son's cheerful help, but also for the grace that allowed *him* to get past his doggedness and initial reluctance to accept the kindness and the goodness that had happened his way.

Surely, we have all had experiences of surprising acts of kindness from unexpected neighbors. I certainly have. Here is a special memory of my own that I will never forget.

Decades ago, I was battling severe depression and anxiety after graduating from college, uncertain of my place in the world and of whether I would ever find a place at all. One Friday afternoon when I was feeling especially discouraged, I jumped impulsively into the car after work and headed east for the Jersey shore. I needed to get away. From earliest childhood, the ocean had always been a healing place for me, and that afternoon healing was what I needed.

I found a motel, walked by the sea . . . But the next morning, while I felt a little calmer, depression and anxiety still haunted me. Aimlessly, I began driving around. And then I saw a sign at the end of a long drive: "Stillwater Studio," it read.

I had brought watercolors with me—another source of balm, I had discovered over the years—and it occurred to me that it might be comforting to check out this studio. So I turned into the drive.

As I approached the house, a lovely middle-aged woman who had been standing at the screen door saw me and came out. I can still visualize her many decades later, with her colorful smock and informal peasant skirt, her thick salt-and-pepper curls, and pendant earrings. But mostly I remember her face: vivid and laughing, and so very, very alive.

"I saw your sign, and . . . Well, I just wondered if I could look at some of your work," I told her. She must have sensed the tension in my voice (how could she not?), and immediately her lovely face was suffused with yet another expression: a deep, essential kindness.

"Of course," she said, and led me into a spacious room whose walls were crowded with watercolors—seascapes, still life studies, and way over in the corner, a painting she was evidently working on now: a picture of a simple wooden table on which stood a bright blue ceramic vase filled with graceful sea grass and sea oats, and next to it a gnarled branch of gray driftwood.

"Oh, they're so beautiful." It escaped from me in a kind of rush, a sigh. And then suddenly I was talking to her as though she were a confidante, an old friend. "I love watercolors so much," I heard myself saying. "In fact, I even brought some paints with me this weekend, just in case I found something. You know, maybe a special scene somewhere, something that I wanted to paint."

Immediately she was all enthusiasm. "Look here," she said, eyes sparkling. "Do you have them with you? Out in your car, I mean?" I nodded, and she continued, "Well then, you know what I'd like to do? I'd like to take a look at some of your things, and maybe give you a lesson! Right here, right now. Would you like that?"

"A lesson? Oh, but I'm not that good. And I couldn't . . . Well I couldn't really pay you anything. I'm on a really tight budget. In fact,"—and I smiled a little ruefully—"the money for this trip and the motel I stayed in last night probably used up all my spending money for about the next two months!"

She brushed it off with a laugh. "Don't be silly. I wasn't even thinking of your paying me. I meant just for the fun of it, the two of us. Go on, why don't you get your things? If you'd like to, that is . . ."

Like to? What could I imagine that could be more wonderful? So I went out to the car and soon we were poring over my paintings together while she, in true teacher style, found things to compliment while also pointing out areas where I could learn some new techniques. "Sponge work," she said firmly. "That's what you want to develop. You'll absolutely love what it can do. I can tell from the way you like to paint. It'll help you with all those wonderful skies. And you'll want to practice blocking in the basic shapes first, applying some very light base colors really quickly so that you can paint over them later, after they're completely dry. And then you can fine-tune it with some dry brush work. You'll love that too. Like this . . . See . . . ?"

For half an hour, it was sheer heaven. She gave of herself so completely—to me, a perfect stranger. And then, at the end, she embraced me warmly. "You have a good weekend now! Go and find some ocean scene that you really love, and practice what we've been doing here." And she sent me on my way.

Were all my problems solved as a result of that encounter? No, of course they weren't. But a real grace touched me that morning. The world was suddenly full of new possibilities for happiness, beauty, and creativity that had scarcely seemed to exist the night before.

Truly, she had become my caring neighbor. Simply because I had happened across her path and she had sensed my pain.

Don't many of us know people like this? We can find them on all sides—at work, in church, around the community—folks who seem just by virtue of who they are to be ready to offer themselves to the need at hand. My friend June is exactly like this. No matter what is required, she is so warm and open-hearted that I know I can ask for impromptu assistance with any random task.

Or take Jean, whose generous spirit prompts her to reach out with uncanny sensitivity to anyone in pain whom God places in her path. I think of the stranger who asked if Jean knew where yarn and knitting supplies might be shelved in the huge department store where they both happened to be shopping. That random encounter turned into a ten minute conversation during which, as Jean asked a question here and a question there, the woman ended up sharing her grief over a friend's terminal illness and was so moved by Jean's compassion that she left in grateful tears, thanking Jean for having made her day.

Then there is Rich, a wonderful man in our church who seems always ready to respond to community emails seeking help—with packing a truck, perhaps, or providing a ride when someone's car has broken down, or doing any one of a hundred other tasks. How well I remember the time that I needed help moving a sofa out of the upstairs apartment I had built above my little ranch house. It was the dead of winter, and I can still see Rich balancing himself precariously as he made his way across the icy deck floor and down the slippery wooden steps, gripping the railing with his right hand and the sofa with his left. What would I have done without him?

Finally, some people serving in particular ministries are so caring in their own right, apart from the roles they happen to be filling, that it is impossible to watch them without marveling at how "being a neighbor" constitutes their very identity. Darleen and her husband Peter are exactly like this. For many years they have given themselves unstintingly to the "Gap Program," College Church's most recent cold weather ministry to the homeless, which offers hot breakfasts and warm hospitality to folks in the early morning hours between seven a.m., when the city's seasonal shelter closes, and ten a.m., when its drop-in day program is open. Besides providing "Gap" breakfasts and engaging in crucial conversations with guests, Darleen and Peter can often be found cruising the downtown streets on the lookout for homeless friends and neighbors for whom they have collected boots, warm socks, or parkas. And they are not the only ones. Many other "Gap" volunteers have also been true neighbors, like Carol and Anne, who have both served as leaders in the past.

So indeed, many people seem naturally to "be neighbors," reaching out to help almost instinctively. But if we look more closely, we can also see people "becoming neighbors" more gradually, as they tap into inner resources like their gifts, joy, and areas of pain.

NEIGHBOR-LOVE GROWS
THROUGH GIFTS AND JOY

Often when people are deeply in touch with their areas of giftedness and the joy those gifts bring them, this seems to happen quite spontaneously. Perhaps this is how it was with that wonderful artist who offered me a free water color lesson during my time of pain. Sometimes, though, people may recognize the importance of their gifts over time, first as they embrace the joy those gifts bring them, and later as they grow into the modes of service they are best suited to offer.

In *Journey Inward, Journey Outward*, Elizabeth O'Connor shares a moving story of how one man at Washington, DC's ecumenical Church of the Saviour found himself unable to enter into any creative ministry with others until he first accepted what brought *him* true joy. For years he had been trying to make himself do the things he thought he *should* do, until one day he asked himself what he actually *wanted* to do. That question ultimately led him to set up a studio and bronze-casting factory in the leaky one room garage which came to double as his home after he embarked on his new life.

Significantly, his decision to honor the God given desires of his heart liberated him to make material sacrifices which formerly would have been unthinkable. And before long, he found that God was guiding him to use his gift on behalf of others; he became a teacher of sculpture in one of the church's missions, the Potter's House Workshop. Experiences like this demonstrate the importance of Church of the Saviour's longtime emphasis on helping its members develop the gifts that bring them joy—gifts that will be used by God for the good of the whole when a person has properly discerned his or her true call.[1]

If we look around our own faith communities, many of us can probably see examples of this principle at work. One of the most dramatic illustrations here in Northampton, Massachusetts, where I live, is evident at the "Manna Community Kitchen" in St. John's Episcopal Church, where Lee serves as director and full-time chef, attracting and inspiring crowds of volunteers to help him prepare and serve the hundreds of magnificently crafted meals that Manna offers every day to the diverse folks who come through their doors. In a recent *Food and Faith* podcast Lee shared with listeners how he first came to this work.[2]

He probably never would have become involved with Manna at all, Lee speculates, were it not for the urging of his friend Dick, who recognized early on Lee's special gift when it came to cooking, and encouraged him to share that with the community. "After all," Dick pointed out, "you not only love to cook; you're really good at it!"

Lee had first taken an interest in cooking as a young man, selling cash registers to the owners of restaurants. On these sales trips he became intrigued by the care people took as they prepared the meals for their customers, but it wasn't until a bit later that he began to practice cooking himself. Visiting his parents' dysfunctional home at holiday times, Lee realized that by offering to do the cooking himself, he could "be there but not be there" as he hung out in the kitchen over a hot stove that others were only too

1. O'Connor, *Journey Inward, Journey Outward,* 33–35.
2. Woofenden and Weston, "Friends at the Table."

happy to relinquish. In stark contrast, Lee was going to find when he joined Manna that his motivation to isolate would be joyously transformed into an open-hearted desire to create beautiful meals for a loving community of goodwill and mutual caring.

Manna's guidelines are all designed to provide fellowship and dignity to folks who have too little of those things in their lives. The street is a cold, hard place to call home, after all; people standing on the sidewalk in hopes of some spare change often find their "invisibility" brought home to them as pedestrians pass by, awkwardly averting their eyes. By contrast, Manna offers a warm welcome, inviting people to come in and be just as they are. If folks want to share their stories, volunteers are ready to lend a listening ear with no hint of judgment, but if people prefer to sit in silence, that is fine too. Guests and volunteers gather together around tables brimming with restaurant quality food that a lot of people can scarcely believe they are receiving. The main goal is to make everyone feel cared for, comfortable, and respected. Why have rigid rules? Lee realized early on. Why let people in only at a specified hour if keeping the doors closed till then means that folks have to stand outside waiting in the rain? The motto "Do no harm" governs it all, together with its corollary, "Do not re-traumatize."

I find it so inspiring to reflect on Lee's journey—especially when I think about Dick's role in first urging him to join the Manna program. Amazingly, it wasn't until Dick's funeral, listening to many others in the congregation sharing how Dick had recognized *their* gifts and pointed them to *their* callings, that Lee realized Dick's *own* gift was to discern and encourage the gifts of others! To be able to do this for so many people, and to watch the fruits of that overflowing in so many lives, must have brought Dick himself great joy.

NEIGHBOR-LOVE GROWS THROUGH PAIN

So yes, recognizing our gifts that bring us joy, and embracing visions that emerge from this, can be one pathway leading us to become neighbors to those around us. But of course, that isn't the only way this can happen. If the capacity to serve often springs from joy, it also grows in places of pain. Sometimes it may actually be our deepest experiences of sorrow and loss, terror and despair, that—years later—we can recognize as the source of our present compassion and empathy. If joy often provides the vitality, pain can enable us to connect on a deeper level with the sufferings of others.

This is why it is important that we be familiar—even comfortable, if possible—with our own painful experiences. If we are, then we will be less likely to put up defenses against our neighbors' struggles when those stir suppressed memories of our own, or to find ourselves projecting onto other people attitudes stemming from our own buried pain. If we have come to a place where we can live at ease with memories of our own areas of suffering, we will be able to hear people more comfortably and clearly as they share their burdens with us. We will be able to give the neighbors whom God sends to us the space simply to *be*.

Writing this reminds me of my friend Faith, a beautiful woman who is now deceased but whose life was a rare gift to many in our church community who were blessed by her compassion. Faith became a neighbor in a very deep way when she chose to make her lovely home in the country available as a place of retreat for people who needed time apart from the pressures of their lives.

Faith was a tiny woman, diminutive and unassuming, by nature extremely shy. And she had a hard life. She was abused emotionally and sexually as a child, remembered hiding in the closet back in the days before she received healing from God for her deep-rooted fears.

If her childhood was hard, though, her marriage was not to be any easier. For years she gave everything she had to make it work, this essentially incompatible union that grew more so over time, especially when she began to draw closer to God and her husband, uncomfortable with this conversion, started to pull away. Finally, he left entirely. What Faith had feared most—the tragedy of divorce—was upon her.

She looked around her house one day. Her three children were grown, her husband was gone. "I should sell this place," she thought. "I should get an apartment. This is too large for a woman alone." Something stopped her, though. It was, she sensed, the voice of God. "No," he seemed to be saying. "You are not to leave your home. I am going to use it. And I am also going to use you."

Use her home? Use her? What could it mean? Faith shared it tentatively with her daughters. "Well," they reminded her, "in a way the house has been used already. Think of how many people have come to you over the years and how you've been able to help them." And yes, it was true. The girls had brought their friends home frequently; one had even moved in for a period of time. It had fulfilled Faith deeply, mothering these hurting young people. "It's all I've ever wanted," she confided to me once. "To be a person who could nurture others, comfort them, help them grow and heal."

Shortly after her daughters pointed out the ways she had already done this, something important happened. A new friend from church, who had recently been abandoned by her own husband and was agonizing over problems with her young son, came at Faith's invitation to spend the weekend. Faith recalls that she brought with her a yellow legal pad crowded with questions about all the life decisions she needed to make. That weekend—over delicious home-cooked meals, talks on the porch by the brook, hours upstairs in a lovely guest room overlooking the woods—Faith and her friend explored and prayed over those questions one by one. Not only did her visitor have a breakthrough experience of healing for herself as a result of their time together, but she gave Faith back something precious in return; she articulated, for her, her *call*.

Faith's eyes shone as she described it. "She helped me see that what I had done for her that weekend, I could really do for others as well. That I had, perhaps, a real ministry—that God had given me a special gift to discern which of my experiences could bring insight to others, and a special opportunity to open my house and my life to people in crisis. That God was inviting me to give others a sacred space to begin dealing prayerfully with their lives."

Faith's ministry was born in that insight. Many came to her after that, referred by word of mouth. By reaching into her own heart and turning her pain over to God, Faith found a genuine call from the Lord, and a concrete way to live out that call among others.

INTEGRATING OUR INWARD AND
OUTWARD JOURNEYS

Lee's and Faith's ministries exemplify how our areas of giftedness and past struggles with pain can become raw material for subsequent journeys into "neighbor-love" and service to others. Recognizing this principle, Church of the Saviour has emphasized the importance of integrating the "journey inward" (prayer, small worship groups, journaling, Bible study, etc.) with the "journey outward" (concrete service at some point of the world's need), and has carved out structures of ministry and accountability to facilitate its members' growth. (See Elizabeth O'Connor's *Journey Inward, Journey Outward*, especially the Preface.) Anyone seriously interested in pursuing the journey into neighbor-love in a church setting would do well to read O'Connor's books that share this community's discoveries. Written a number of years ago, they still remain real treasures of guidance and inspiration. But it is certainly not necessary for individuals or groups to model themselves after this church in all respects, for the principles involved are so basic and scriptural that they can be lived out by any group of believers in a variety of contexts.

Some people may live into such fruitful ministries as they integrate their inward and outward journeys that they wind up being widely recognized for their service. Bill, who worships right here at College Church, is a prime example of this. Now retired, Bill long served as Head Counselor and Program Coordinator for the Substance Abuse Treatment Program at our local Veterans Administration hospital. He is a man whose whole identity has been shaped by his experiences of becoming and being a neighbor to others, thanks to God's work in his life.

It started many decades ago when Bill, who had been seeking escape from an underlying sense of emptiness through drugs and alcohol, found his life falling apart. His marriage broke up. His work was in shambles. Discouraged and alone, he finally admitted that he needed help and determined to seek it. "And God not only directed me to people who could help me begin to get my own life together," he told me, "but he opened my eyes to deeper dreams in my heart.

As I moved into recovery and began to work the program, I started looking around at the many other people who were being helped there, and I thought: 'Wow! This is what I want to do!'

"There was one friend I had—another client in the program—and we had a conversation one day that really made an impact on me. 'You seem awfully invested in the program, awfully connected,' I told him, and he replied that yes, he was. And then he added, 'It's because I've found Christ.'

"'You go to church?' I asked. 'Yes, I do,' he replied, 'but that's not what I'm talking about. I'm talking about a lot more than just that. I'm talking about a relationship.'"

Well that conversation really blew Bill away. So now he had two things to think about: his deepening desire to be of service to others, and his growing pull toward a closer connection with Christ, the kind that his friend had described.

Finally, about a year into his newfound sobriety, after much work and growth in prayer, Bill felt called to take a new step and confided his longings to another person. "I was scared," he acknowledged, "afraid that I might be told I wasn't ready." But he screwed up his courage to approach one of his counselors and to tell this man of his dreams.

The counselor studied him thoughtfully. "Yes," he said. "Yes, I think you've got what it takes. Spiritually you're a lot closer to Christ now, and I think you're ready to begin building on that."

Bill started quietly at first. He began to immerse himself in volunteer work of a humble servant nature—whatever needed doing. At the VA hospital he began to push patients around. At a local Community Action Commission, he helped set up a swap shop. At church he went to AA meetings regularly and began to ask what he could do to help. Setting up food; preparing the coffee; anything that was suggested, he was ready to do it.

The result was amazing. "Wow!" he recalled. "It was really like a miracle. I remember an elderly gentleman in AA saying that to get good quality sobriety you have to give it away, and I saw this more and more. I began talking to all the people I met who were struggling, sharing with them where I was whenever I felt it would help them. Oh, it felt so good! I had a sponsor, I remember, who was also very involved in AA and who played the organ at a church in Springfield, and he said to me, 'Whenever you help someone else, as soon as possible afterwards, get in touch with how *you* feel, because that inner response in your own heart, that's what's really important. That's the driving force. Otherwise you'll soon begin to lose interest.' Well, I always remembered that. When you begin to feel the joy of knowing God is guiding you, putting people into your life, and saying to you, 'That's right,'—well, that's what really keeps you Christ-centered and on the right track. That's what has kept me going."

The deeper Bill immersed himself in service, the more the doors began to open. Today he is widely recognized both locally and nationally for his effectiveness in helping others, and a local halfway house—Hairston House—bears his name in tribute. But you would never guess the awards and accolades he has been given from his modest demeanor. For Bill has an authentic servant's heart—one that has been shaped and nurtured over the years by God's gracious hand in his life.

A MINISTRY TO THE HOMELESS UNFOLDS

There are too many stories to tell them all, but I cannot close this chapter without sharing a bit more about how I began to discover the principles of becoming a neighbor in my own life, when I got involved, several decades ago, in volunteer work with homeless men and women.

Homelessness . . . The very word, these many years later, stirs memories of the anguish and terror I felt when my marriage crashed in divorce, and I was forced to leave the house my former husband and I had built together, forced to strike out into an uncertain world as a single-again woman, uprooted from everything that had defined my identity and my place in life. I was not really homeless, to be sure; I had settlement money in the bank, sufficient to last for a year or so if I didn't get work immediately, and I also had a temporary place to live, an apartment in Cambridge which a friend had offered to sublet to me while she began a transitional move of her own to New York City. Still, the trauma was very real.

As I lay there in Cynthia's apartment the radio was often on in the background, and I couldn't help noticing that one issue came up again and again on the local news: condo conversions; gentrification; escalating rents. There in the city of Boston people who had formerly rented their homes—the elderly, in many cases—were being put out onto the streets as their meager funds proved insufficient to secure new housing in a rapidly changing real estate market. It was the beginning of what was soon to become an epidemic of ravaging proportions.

Would this be my fate too? I found myself agonizing, as I lay on Cynthia's daybed in that tiny studio apartment. How long would my money last? Maybe a year? How could I predict what would happen to me? What if I couldn't find an appropriate job? What if, what if . . .? It was a wild, irrational terror.

I was a new Christian at the time, having recently experienced Jesus' love breaking over me in awesome ways at the time my marriage was crumbling. Perhaps this is why even in the midst of my anxiety something in me still sensed that the day might come when God would use these experiences for some eventual good I could not as yet foresee . . .

It would be several years before that happened, though. First, I went through a period of struggle and loneliness. Moving back to western Massachusetts, I began to rebuild my life from the ground up,—settling into a new job, buying a little house—all the while holding Jesus' challenges at bay, yet knowing that eventually I must face them. Then at last I began to realize that I was finally becoming ready to shift my focus from my own anxious concerns to the needs and concerns of others. Interestingly, I can pinpoint quite precisely the day that the turning point came; it was the day that I met Jessie Benoit.

Jessie—"Mom" to the many people who knew and loved her—at that time owned and operated a twenty-four-hour diner in town, a haven for the down-and-out, where the hungry could always find a sandwich and a cup of coffee, where former mental patients could find a listening ear, and where the homeless could find a surrogate family. The city's shelter for homeless families—Jessie's House—had been named after her.

As I sat at the counter of Jessie's diner where I went one day to seek her out, Jessie and I fell into a long conversation. She had recently been hospitalized, and her exhaustion was apparent. Bobby pins secured errant strands of gray hair she had pulled back from her damp forehead, and she moved with an air of heavy tiredness as she told me how someone had conned her out of a meal the previous night. But then abruptly her mood changed as she pressed some photographs into my hand. "These are my grandchildren," she said proudly. "Aren't they cute? Look at those grins!"

That afternoon was so important to me, and I found myself so moved by Jessie's pluck, compassion, and simple endurance, that before long I had embarked on a new adventure of my own. I became a volunteer at Jessie's House myself.

It turned out to be a hectic, chaotic, rich-hearted place. There was a swirl of jangling telephones and chattering toddlers; there were folks coming and going to donate casseroles and clothing, or to secure Salvation Army vouchers for a bus ride to the next city. Everybody—guests, staff, volunteers—worked together like a huge extended family bonded by a special caring and warmth. That was a crucial time for me, the period that I was there. Then a year or so later I became involved in issues of homelessness more deeply as I found myself, along with Pastor Dave McDowell and others, setting up an emergency shelter program at College Church to take in the men and women Jessie's House had to turn away for lack of space on cold winter nights.

It felt like God's perfect timing as resources poured in, in response to our call. Amazing numbers of people streamed forward to help: to spend the night, to offer linens and blankets, to do the laundry. The Red Cross loaned us a large supply of cots, and Jessie's House staff agreed to be our screening consultants.

How odd it is to remember that in those days five guests seemed to us like a crowd! For before long, tragically, the crisis had escalated to the point where we housed an average of fourteen or fifteen people a night and fed twice as many as that in our "soup kitchen," the supper component of the program that soon came into being. It is exponentially worse today, of course. But if it was heartbreaking to see the proliferating need, there were rewards too, as so many people, including folks from other churches in town, became involved in the effort. Eventually the city responded by opening a year-round shelter for single people, and as other resources moved into place as well, our individual cot program was disbanded.

Those of us who had set this whole process in motion soon found ourselves changing in important ways. Gathered around the card table in the room behind the sanctuary that served as our in-take area, we all began opening up to one another—volunteers and guests alike—and sharing our stories and struggles with a comfort and spontaneity we might not have expected.

For myself, I could only marvel at what a difference it was making in my own life. From a place of relative isolation in the church, I was moving into community; from a place of theological confusion over differences in doctrine, I was moving into a shared enterprise of caring and concern; from a place of personal loneliness, I was moving into a new fabric of relationship and involvement; and from a place where my own painful memories were locked away in secret, I was learning to share the lessons they had taught me. Always I felt close to Jesus in a special way there in the shelter. In becoming a neighbor to others, I was discovering a whole new sense of myself.

HOW BECOMING A NEIGHBOR
TRANSFORMS OUR HEARTS

How does this happen? How do relationships with our neighbors gradually transform our hearts? It must have something in common with the growth that occurs in more conventional relationships when over time, in healthy friendships and families, we develop more mature ways of caring and learn to let go of egocentric patterns. The difference is that with neighbor-love there is no prior personal relationship; we simply start at the outset with intentional "agape love" (what C. S. Lewis refers to as "charity" in *The Four Loves*[3]) and let God take it from there.

Some might ask if these are really "love relationships" that we have in such cases. The answer, it seems to me, is a solid *yes*. Isn't

---

3. Lewis, *The Four Loves*, 181–87.

this implicit in the second great commandment, "Love your neighbor as yourself"? The point is that this is a special sort of love. It is the kind of love the Samaritan showed to the man who had fallen into the robbers' hands.

The Samaritan had compassion. Out of other-directed concern for the beaten man's practical needs, he made the intentional choice to extend himself and become involved. We can all make such intentional choices. Each one of us has the opportunity to enter into relationships of neighbor-love, for God has placed these potential neighbors in our lives on every side, waiting only for us to come forward in response. Neighbor-love is one human relationship that is absolutely gratuitous. Opening ourselves to this process, we will discover how it feels, deep in the heart, to *become neighbors* ourselves.

REFLECTIVE QUESTIONS: CHAPTER 2

1. Remember a time when someone met you compassionately at a place of emotional, practical, or spiritual need. How did you feel before that encounter? How did you feel afterwards? What was it about the other person's actions or presence that made the biggest difference?

2. Can you identify areas of your own giftedness? Try to think about both your "natural gifts," with which you were born, and your "spiritual gifts," bestowed by the Holy Spirit so you can nourish and strengthen the body of Christ. If you are uncertain about your spiritual gifts, you may wish to ask for input from your pastor or from close Christian friends. See also 1 Corinthians 12:4–11, Romans 12:4–8, and Ephesians 4:11–13. Bring the matter of your gifts to God in prayer. Ask God and others who know you well to help you see how you might use your gifts on behalf of others.

3. What brings you joy? Have you found ways to contribute to others' lives by sharing this joy with them? How might you do this more often and more creatively?

4. What have been some of your encounters with pain, both in your own experience and in the experiences of people you love? In general, are you are able to let yourself feel your pain, or do you defend yourself against it by trying to deny it, distract yourself, or stuff it down? When you are with others who are suffering, do you generally feel able simply to "be there" with and for them, or do you usually feel a need to "fix" their pain without fully listening, to make it go away?

5. Who do you know who most embodies neighbor-love? How does this person make you feel, and why?

Chapter 3

The Neighborly Community

Sometimes when we try to help another person, we find that we just can't do it alone. Haven't we all experienced times when particular relationships have overwhelmed us?

Perhaps it is a problem of communication in which, try as we may, we can't get across some basic truth we are groping to express. Or maybe it is a question of limited time and seemingly unlimited demands, a mounting sense of frustration and irritation as we chafe over the pressures this person is placing on us. It may even be that our benevolence is being actively abused, as someone cynically takes the help we offer while willfully continuing to behave in a destructive or self-destructive fashion.

Whatever the circumstances, at times like this we need the perspective and help of others. We need to come together with folks who share our concern for the individual who is draining us and for the larger problems his or her situation poses. We need to bear one another's burdens, to pool our perceptions, to reach out together in prayer with the special power that comes when "two or three" are gathered in Jesus' name.

WHEN OUR NEIGHBORS' NEEDS
CREATE COMMUNITY

A few years after we had set up our emergency shelter at College Church, a group of us learned some exciting lessons about the difference that sharing and praying together can make in pursuing a common ministry. How did it happen? When did it begin? Looking back on it now, I think that for me, at least, it all began in mounting frustration over Willard.

Willard. How to describe him? And how to describe what he meant to us? Somewhere in his seventies, Willard was sinewy and tough and rugged as a walnut shell, with his khaki pants and pale blue windbreaker and battered denim cap, permanently perched at a rakish angle with wisps of white-blond hair escaping from under its brim. When he talked, Willard released the words slowly, deliberately—almost reluctantly—as if afraid that he might release along with them some private secret he wasn't sure he wanted the world to know. Head tipped back, eyes half closed, Willard often seemed far away, focused on some inner vision of his own. But he also had—no doubt about it—a glint of mischief in his eyes, a chuckle in his voice. His body would tilt sideways as he balanced his weight between his good right leg and his artificial left one, feet planted square apart for stability like someone on the deck of a storm-tossed ship. Even without knowing the details, you could tell Willard had been through a lot. A survivor, that's what he was. Willard was your quintessential survivor.

He was our very first guest, the first ever to come to our shelter. I remember watching him from my car that evening as he puttered around in his, collecting plastic bags with toothbrush, papers, and assorted belongings, getting ready to come in and join us for the night. He ended up with us again many times off and on over the years, till we came to know him as you know one of the family: a brother, an uncle, a cousin. And just as with family, at various times all of us felt for him affection, annoyance, joy, frustration, and love.

Willard.

You should have heard him break out into singing at six in the morning, exercising his lungs with a powerhouse rendition of

"You'll Never Walk Alone." Or you should have seen him doing his push-ups at five a.m., with all the resolution and stamina of a thirty-five-year-old.

But oh, so stubborn! Just try to get Willard to change his mind about something! You would be in for a tug of war you never could have anticipated, a battle of wills like nothing you've ever known.

During the day many of our shelter guests would frequent the library where I worked before taking off at night for supper in the church and cots behind the sanctuary. Willard was one. There he'd sit in the library's reading room, small notebook filled with what appeared to be shorthand scribbles, a littered pile of clippings and papers surrounding his spot. Sweepstakes entry forms. Crossword puzzles. Astrology notes. Xerox copies of endless correspondence. Pursuing his affairs till supper time rolled around.

When it was time to leave, my supervisor at the library (another Elise!) would often take turns with me driving him over to the church before we headed home ourselves. For by this time Willard's car was permanently grounded in the church's parking lot with some ailment that never quite seemed repairable, while the snow piled up over it and the snowplow navigated around its bulk as best it could. Now, all this was tolerable for a time. But then it began to get more complicated.

Willard wanted to be driven when *he* wanted to be driven. Not before, not after. And sometimes our schedules just didn't dovetail, especially on Mondays—my long day, when I worked from nine in the morning till nine at night, except for lunch and supper breaks. That supper hour was precious to me. Exhausted from the day's demands, I wanted only to go home, turn on the TV, and collapse on the couch for a few blessed moments before facing the evening shift.

But then there was Willard, never quite ready when I needed to leave. ("W-a-a-a-l-l . . . It's really *better* for me, don't you know, if we wait till six-twenty-five." "But Willard, I have to leave *now*.") Interminably, it felt, this little scene would play itself out week after week, I too exhausted to set firm limits, while the emotional temperature—on my part at least—was rising dangerously. One night I heard myself say, really angrily by then, after we had finally driven over to the church and I was reaching across in front of him to open the door on the passenger side and let him out, "*Willard, the trouble with you is that you just will not realize other people have schedules they need to keep, as well as you!*" When at last he had made his way out onto the church driveway, I slammed the door hard after him and roared away, angrily gunning the engine.

Well, it was an appropriate thing to have said to him, wasn't it? And wasn't my anger also appropriate? Then why did I feel so bad afterwards? Why, in fact, did I lie awake over it that night, the sound of my own voice playing itself over and over in my mind's ear?

I didn't find peace till the next morning, when I encountered him making his way up the library walk at the same time that I was leaving my parked car, and we fell into step together. I didn't exactly apologize. It wasn't at all clear to me that an apology was called for. But some sort of reconciliation was in order.

"A nice sunny day, isn't it?" I ventured tentatively.

He allowed as how it was.

A squirrel scampered across the crusted snow in front of us, and we paused to watch it together. "You know," I said, "I was look-ing out my kitchen window the other day and there were three of them chasing each other around and around the trees. They must have chased each other for close to half an hour."

He chuckled then, in that half public, half private way he had. "Yes, they're wonderful little creatures," he agreed. I grinned at him, and suddenly he grinned back. We laughed together. It was all right.

But still, difficulties remained. The thing is, Willard was a problem to people other than me. There was that car of his in the church parking lot, for instance, partially blocking the drive where the snowplow needed to go through. He had promised repeatedly to get it fixed, but even when we made appointments with mechanics for him, offered to pay if need be, somehow it never quite happened. There was his loud style of protest and—occasionally—accompany-ing physical gestures for added emphasis when he perceived some invasion of his turf at the shelter. There was his peculiar ability to stick to his own view of an issue, to dig in his heels against any al-ternative interpretation, no matter how hard we were trying—with increasing frustration—to explain it to him. Yes, no doubt about it; Willard was a problem.

Finally, for a variety of reasons, we made an administrative decision. At long last we needed to enforce a rule that limited a guest's stay at the shelter when attendance was pushing capacity and others needed the space. But of course, we were not going to turn this elderly man out into the snow. So, a kind of ad hoc group came together, quite informally and unofficially, to find alternative arrangements for Willard.

Two of us were from the church program itself. Then there was Cathy, the coordinator of Jessie's House; Susan, a social worker helping us with our program; and Elise, my supervisor at the library and co-driver for Willard.

Now, as we met together to share our concerns, our frustrations, and yes, our *dreams* for Willard, something quite remarkable started to happen. Swapping stories and memories, giving vent to some of the annoyance that had built up over the months, we found that increasingly we were all feeling a great affection for this man who had brought us together, and a real closeness among ourselves.

"He was my roommate once, you know," Cathy volunteered. "It was a kind of commune run by one of the Amherst churches. I really got to know his patterns there . . . Oh, my!" And she laughed to herself at the memory.

"I've done my best to explain things to him, my very best. Really, I have." This was Susan now. "But he just will not listen to reason!"

"Oh well, that's Willard!" Cathy's sense of the comic had risen to the fore now as it often did when she bumped up against unexpected hurdles in the day's routine. She laughed again. And suddenly, the rest of us found that we were laughing with her.

We went on to think of possible game plans. First, we needed to get that car fixed, if possible. And of course, he needed a place to sleep. The Salvation Army shelter in Greenfield would do for now; he could stay there indefinitely while we explored other possibilities here. "You know,"—Cathy's voice was suddenly excited—"I think Willard should have an apartment in the elderly housing complex here! He'd be the perfect candidate. He's homeless; he's physically handicapped. He could get a place in two weeks. I'm positive of it! Oh, but would he take it? He's been homeless so long, it would be a whole different world for him. Could he make that adjustment?" We went round and round with it; we weren't sure.

Finally, Cathy said with resolution, "I know what I'm going to do. I'm going to put Willard right here in my prayer jar. Right now." She pointed to a little ceramic vase in which she placed scraps of paper with the names of people in Jessie's House who were up against what seemed insurmountable odds. She grabbed a piece of paper and a pencil, scribbled his name, and dropped it in the jar. "There!" she announced. "This one calls for a miracle!"

Glory to God, the miracle came through. After a couple of months at the Greenfield shelter where we had driven him for the interim, Willard's name came up on the list. He was given his apartment.

Would he like it? Would he accept it? We all waited at Jessie's House, collectively breathless, till he met us on the designated morning with Susan, having taken a preliminary look at the apartment. As soon as we saw his face—sparkling eyes, an expression almost of awe—we knew that it was going to be all right.

In fact, it was even more than all right. He had loved it! The parquet floors . . . the screened-in porch . . . He and I talked in the hall as Cathy frantically vacuumed the living room of Jessie's House, shooed kids away, and shoved chairs into place for our official meeting. Then she was ready for us, and we all trooped in.

Willard sat down in the big armchair and turned toward us. He beamed.

"It's a *beautiful* place. *Bee-ooo-ti-ful!*" He chuckled, nodded his head toward Cathy, who was so bursting with joy by now that she was joking, giggling, nearly hysterical, barely able to contain her gratitude and relief. "A bull's eye, that's what!" Willard continued. "She was right on target this time. A real bull's eye! Yes, siree!"

And now Cathy could remain silent no longer. "So, what do you think of this, Willard?" she asked. "You know, Willard, I was afraid we were almost going to lose this one. I put your name into my prayer vase. That's what I do when something's outside my own control. I said to God, 'Now look here, God, you're going to have to watch out for Willard on this one, you hear? Peer down into that little vase, God! Say, "That's my Willard in there! I see him! I'm going to do something myself, now, to fix this up".'"

Willard chortled, delighted. "So, God was looking down into a vase . . . Hey, that's rich, that one! So is God a Frenchman, looking around corners?" He chuckled again.

Cathy shook her finger at him, a mock schoolteacher. "Oh, but Willard, he did look out for you now, didn't' he? He really did! This is a little miracle, Willard, that's exactly what this is!" And then, finally, we moved on to the specifics of business.

"Let's see. What will you need? Let's make some lists. Okay, you'll need a table, a chair, a bed. We can get that from the Salvation Army."

"A bed. You mean a cot."

"No, no, Willard. Not one of those rickety old canvas cots. Not like the one you've been sleeping on at the shelter. No, I mean a real bed. *Your very own bed, with a roll-up mattress!*

"Okay. And you'll probably want something that makes sound. So, you won't be lonely. A TV? A radio?"

"There will be lots of tag sales this weekend." This was my contribution, now, for tag sales are one of my favorite things. "I can find a nice little radio for you, I'm sure, and maybe a TV too. How about pots, pans? Anything else for the kitchen?"

"A tea kettle. That's what I want. And a nice solid standing lamp . . ."

"Okay, I'll get them."

I found them all. The first TV didn't have very good sound, but I bought it anyway,—it was just two dollars—then found a better one later for three, and left the first with the sellers, as a donation. Then I saw the perfect lamp. I had a real struggle of conscience over that. It happened to be exactly what I had been looking for, for my own living room. Oh, could I keep it? He'd never know! And I was already taking him so much . . . But no, of course I took him the lamp as well, that afternoon. God had provided it for him, hadn't he? Only by then, Willard's mood was beginning to change.

He'd had several days to sit around in that sterile, empty apartment, like a fish out of water. And when I came in and brought the furniture, I found a very different man than the one I had left on Wednesday afternoon.

"Look here," he said to me. "Sit down. I've got to talk to you." I sat. Long pause. And then he launched in.

"Hey, look here. This just isn't right, y'know? This isn't how I'm used to living. I'm used to living outside. I'm used to bathing in icy mountain streams, cold like fire, eating tuna out of a can. No, I'm not sure this was such a good idea. This is no place for me."

Well, I knew what he meant. But of course, it had never been our idea that he would *belong* in this conventional, secure apartment, with the old ladies whispering together downstairs, gossiping across the hall. We had seen it as a seasonal bed, pure and simple, a place to be in out of the cold. I tried to explain this.

"Willard, you don't have to spend all your time here. You can do all the things and go out to all the places you always used to. You can still come have supper with us at the church, still spend days at the library. And in the summer, you can take off for the mountains if you like, spend months there in the woods in your trailer." (He had a trailer somewhere off in the Berkshires; no one knew quite where. All we knew was that it wasn't habitable in the winter, which was why the ice and snow always drove him back down into the Valley, regular as clockwork, like some migratory bird heading south.) "Willard, as long as your SSI pays the rent, you don't have to spend any more time here than you want. But when you do need it, to sleep in when it's cold, then you'll have it. Don't you see?"

But this wasn't enough. I could tell from his expression. I thought of something else. "Willard, you know what? *I* eat tuna out of a can too! I do it all the time. Everyone at the library teases me about it, but it's just something I like to do. It's so quick and easy. If I can do that and still live in a house, you can do that and live in this apartment. Can't you?"

Couldn't he?

Well, maybe we couldn't really convince him for sure ahead of time. Maybe we just needed to wait and see what he would do.

The crisis came a few months later, at the end of June. I got a call at work. It was Cathy, frantic. He'd taken off. He'd handed in his key without even telling any of us. He'd given it up.

What could we do? Desperate, we came together in a huddle once again. "It's the wrong season," Cathy moaned. "That's the whole problem. Oh, if we could just manage to keep it for him till the cold weather sets in, when he has to leave those mountains and come back down here again, then it would make some sense to him, then he'd see it differently."

We began to volunteer ideas.

"Well, I could probably chip in something toward the rent . . ."

"So could I, probably. Not a lot, but some . . ."

"And maybe some churches in town might help out a bit, too. Just to hold it for him a couple of months, till it gets to be fall . . ."

In view of the special circumstances, when we approached the Housing Authority they finally agreed. They would wait a little longer before reassigning the apartment, provided that we, as a group, made sure the rent was paid.

The only person who didn't know about this was Willard. And we didn't know where *he* was!

A couple of months later we found him. Susan had bumped into him in Greenfield one day and they had fallen into conversation. The apartment? Well, actually it was still there for him, if he wanted it, she explained. The group had decided to cover the rent.

I didn't see his response, so I can't describe the look on his face. But Susan reported his words to us. "Hmmmmm . . . Hrrummph . . . W-a-a-l-l-l . . . You know, I wondered if something like that might not have been going on . . ."

You wondered . . . Yes, Willard, for you were getting to know us by then. You knew on some level how much we all cared about you, even though you often made us so very frustrated! You knew that we couldn't let you throw that place away till you had a chance to realize what you were doing.

What did it mean to him, that we did that? It must have meant something, because almost immediately he was back. He came to Jessie's House the very next day, met with Cathy, and worked out an arrangement whereby he would get the rent paid automatically each month out of his SSI check. And yes, he stuck to it. He didn't come to supper at the church over the next couple of years, as we had hoped he might ("Well, I'm very *busy*, don't you know?"), and he didn't frequent the library quite so often. But he still came in now then, and his eyes still twinkled. He still wore the same pants, the same windbreaker, with his cap still tilted at that rakish angle. He showed us the envelope he was preparing for the sweepstakes, his Publishers Clearing House stickers and forms. He even came in with a request one day just like old times. "Hmmmmm," he began. "Do you know anyone who might have a three by six table and about six chairs? I want them so I can have some people to dinner."

I laughed out loud then. "Willard, you know that if you do that, we'll have to be the first people you ask!"

He laughed too, then grinned. "Well, of course."

In a couple of weeks, the table and chairs were located and delivered, donated by a member of the church. When I saw Willard again shortly after that to deliver a bookcase—his most recent request—the table and chairs stood in place, all set up in the living room, piled high with his papers. It looked as if Willard was finally settling in, finally beginning to feel somewhat at home.

It would be nice to add, "And he lived happily ever after." This is real life though, not a fairytale, and unfortunately as the years rolled on some issues developed, too complicated to detail here, so that ultimately our solution proved unworkable. Still, for several years Willard had the security during cold winter months of a place to call home. More importantly, hopefully he realized that we—and God—truly loved him, in a way he had not understood before.

Something important also happened between those of us who came together to relocate him. In a new and wonderful way, we had become neighbors to one another. In the extremity of our frustration, our inability to cope with Willard all alone, we had become a "neighborly community." Willard had brought us together.

A LOCAL MISSION GROUP GATHERS

Meanwhile, those of us who were involved in the shelter program at College Church, and had been meeting with or hearing about the "Willard group," were struck by the difference it had made as we struggled with our frustrations. Wouldn't it be wonderful if we could have a College Church group like this too, so we could share and pray together over the shelter ministry as a whole? In one sense we already had a group, of course, since periodically our volunteers all met to accomplish specific tasks: decision-making; orientation and training sessions; an occasional "gratitude dinner." We had talked about trying to meet more often—monthly, say, after church—but somehow what with everyone's busy schedule and the chaos of the after-church hour, that never got off the ground.

We needed to do something, though. And there was one occasion in particular when this need became clear.

A few of us had lingered after church one Sunday morning and were discussing the shelter. John, one of our most dedicated volunteers, an undergraduate at the local university, started to voice several questions that had been plaguing him over the past year: about his relationship with God; about inhibitions when it came to sharing his faith with guests; about his struggles with our perennial conflict between justice and mercy at the point of rule enforcement.

We listened, asked questions, encouraged him to share more. And as the conversation unfolded, I became more and more amazed.

All this that he had been carrying inside! Finally, ever so gently, I asked him, "John, I know that you and I haven't had a chance to talk a lot this year, so maybe that's why all this sounds so new to me. But what about with other people? Have you at least had a chance to share some of this with them?"

He looked puzzled, as if that thought hadn't occurred to him. "No, this is the first time. I guess I've just been kind of keeping it all to myself. I mean, I wasn't sure what else to do. After all, we don't often get together in a small group like this, you know. And it's kind of hard otherwise to really find a way to talk about it."

Kind of hard indeed! But so very important.

Probably the most crucial need, once we move a certain distance into helping relationships with others, is for just such a neighborly community, composed of folks with whom we can share burdens, needs, visions, and concerns. At Washington, DC's Church of the Saviour this kind of sharing occurs in what that fellowship has come to call its "mission groups." These groups take shape when folks—as few at first, perhaps, as two or three —discover a common vision to which they feel called and come together to pray over it and bring it into being.[1]

Those of us who were involved in College Church's outreach work with the homeless were surely responding to the Holy Spirit's work in our hearts when, in the wake of that experience with Willard, increasingly we began to ask ourselves questions.

What if we could have a small group of shelter volunteers who would make a mutual commitment to gather together for regular prayer and sharing, say one evening every other week? True, our lives were already too busy, and whenever someone had suggested such a group in the past, it had seemed unrealistic. But . . . Might it be possible?

One morning Pastor Dave voiced it himself to a few of us who were chatting after church. "You know," he said, "it's true that we all have crowded schedules and we've struggled with the idea of committing ourselves to a regular meeting. But what would you think of forming a kind of oversight committee for the shelter this coming fall? Maybe we could meet biweekly to share and pray and plan over what's going on. Then we'd no longer be out there standing alone with our concerns, but we could really be together for mutual support."

And so, our shelter "mission group" was born. What a difference it made! How, I found myself wondering, had we ever managed before? The answer is that we managed only partially. We ricocheted from crisis to crisis, from guest to guest, isolated and fragmented in large measure, coping as best we could. And sometimes it wasn't very well at all.

We needed each other. Now, for the first time, we had a framework to meet that need.

A MISSION GROUP NURTURES ITS MEMBERS

Mark put it this way. "Over time we became trusting enough to allow personal relationships to develop so we could really feel

---

1. O'Connor, *Call to Commitment*, 49.

comfortable sharing some of our struggles together. We were still task oriented enough to do the job, but we found that if one of us was struggling with some issue connected with the ministry, that reduced our effectiveness if it wasn't adequately dealt with. 'There's wisdom in many counselors.' At one point we all spilled our guts to each other, and I know that when I did this, I was really blessed by the way everyone was there to encourage and affirm me."

How true this is! Each of us individually, after all, can only bring our own particular temperaments, attitudes, backgrounds, and predispositions to any ministry in which we serve. We may know one person very well, anther hardly at all. But others can balance out our own reactions and views. As we pool our perspectives—careful to respect necessary confidences, of course—we get a fuller picture of each situation than we ever could have discovered alone. And we learn a great deal about ourselves in the process.

I've never raised children, but after bringing my difficulties with our nineteen-year-old to the group and hearing other people's reactions to the ways I was unwittingly manipulated, I often felt as if I had learned a few of the lessons motherhood might have taught me! You can learn a lot when, in addition to living into neighbor-love on your own, you are also part of a neighborly community.

When we share feelings and come together for intercessory prayer, we learn a lot about our own capacities to love. The experience reminds me of a comment I read once in a book whose title I cannot remember, to the effect that the people you come to love best are the ones you treat as well as you can, not necessarily the ones who treat you well in return. It is true. Choose to take a chance for someone, to go out on a limb, and your love deepens. So, of course, does your vulnerability and your capacity to grieve. This is why, without one another's support, we might find it impossible to extend ourselves so deeply. For there will always be people who abuse your caring, and sometimes that hurts a great deal. At these times folks in a neighborly community can share the pain together, help each other process that pain, and respond more fruitfully than any one person could respond alone.

One morning another volunteer and I were cleaning up in the shelter after our guests had left. We were throwing towels into piles, collecting used sheets, when Edwina suddenly stopped and knelt down. Then she said, her voice very grim, "*Look*," and held out a small pencil-like object.

"What's that?" I asked. I stared at it dumbly, seeing it of course, but refusing to recognize what I was looking at.

"That, my dear," she said—and her voice was very hard—"is a syringe. And . . ." (she held it out again to show me its rusted bit of red at the end of the needle), "*It's been used.*"

Why did it hit me so? Of course, a number of our guests used, as they say; that was no surprise. *But not in the church!* Somehow that felt like such a violation, such a betrayal.

At the next group meeting we began to process it. We had no way of knowing whose it was, and for that, I think, we were grateful. "It's as if God is giving us little doses of reality bit by bit, as we're ready," someone said. "It's like God is saying to us, 'Don't think you can do my work in these dark places and always keep your hands clean. You can't. Sometimes your hands will get dirty. You have to expect that.'"

Obviously, blind naivete is not good for anyone. That was what we were beginning to learn in our group. We were learning to let one person's caution balance another's impulsiveness, one person's reflective thought balance another's deep feeling. We were learning together to be, as Jesus puts it, "as shrewd as snakes and as innocent as doves" (Matthew 10:16).

Yes, we were all learning. And one of the most important lessons was this: that whether or not we were conned, whether or not our caring was abused, whether or not there was a genuine response, a real miracle of transformation, all of that, ultimately, lay outside our control. For us, the rock-bottom reality was that in our acts of obedience, our acts of love and service, we knew we were growing more deeply into the people God wanted us to be. And that obedience was made possible, in large measure, by one another's support and prayer.

A NEIGHBORLY COMMUNITY OFFERS HINTS OF KINGDOM LIVING

"But seek first his kingdom and his righteousness . . ." (Matthew 6:33). Isn't it true, really, that to love our neighbors together, grounded in God and in community with one another, can be a kind of operational definition of what it means to live here and now into God's embryonic kingdom? Surely the closer we come to living out this command with fellow believers in our earthly lives, the more we will experience glimmers and hints of what "kingdom living" will ultimately be like.

When we minister as a corporate body in this way, we must surrender many of our personal preferences and agendas almost of necessity, if the work of the whole group is to move forward under God's guidance. Deep surrender to the Lord—total openness to seek and to follow God's direction—can be a struggle for many of us (I speak from experience!), but when we are inspired by a common vision and strengthened by mutual bonds of prayerful support, then amazing things can happen. We may find that we are suddenly able to trust God in more daring ways than we are usually able do in our private personal lives. As we venture out in faith, caring and praying for others together, the kinds of risky steps we might sometimes avoid individually can become a lot easier. We can be awed at the way God works in our midst.

Experiences like this bring joy, for they give us hints of what gospel trust is really all about, and what Jesus means when he invites us to find our lives by losing them—in him.

REFLECTIVE QUESTIONS: CHAPTER 3

1. Are you worried about a situation that someone in your church community is facing but feel hesitant to seek the guidance of others by sharing details involved, or to pray over the issue in a small group without your friend being present, lest you violate his or her privacy? Could you consider asking your friend to join you and other concerned individuals for a time

of shared prayer, so that you could all come together before God about the issue at hand?

2. If you are involved in volunteer work or in some ministry through your church, think about the other people you know who are engaged in that same effort. How well do you know one another? How deep is your level of mutual trust? Do you feel free to be vulnerable together as you share personal feelings? If not, how might you begin to strengthen mutual trust? Pray over this question and seek God's guidance.

3. Choose a group of people with whom you are familiar in your faith community (members of a prayer group or Bible study, say, or a small group ministry). Reflect on the members of this group as you read 1 Corinthians 12. Can you identify gifts exhibited by the men and women in your chosen group? Beyond specific areas of giftedness mentioned in this passage, what qualities among folks in your group are helpful to your common enterprise, and what ones create obstacles? How do you see your own role in the group? Ask others to share with you how they see your role.

4. Come together with a group of others for a period of shared "listening prayer." First, identify together some question of common concern. Second, have someone voice this concern aloud in prayer. Third, spend ten or fifteen minutes in silence, all listening together for God's guidance. And fourth, share with one another any insights you each may have received.

5. Search the New Testament for some examples of small group conflicts (for instance, in Mark 10:35–45) and the ways Jesus deals with them in the gospels, or Paul responds in his epistles. Can you recognize any patterns of interaction which you also see in your own church community or small group? Invite others to consider this as well, and share responses.

PART TWO

My Self

Chapter 4

Selfhood and Identity

"*Love your neighbor as* yourself," Jesus tells us in Matthew 22:39. But how does God want us to love ourselves? Answers to this question vary with the individuals who offer them, but in my experience, they often tend to converge around one of two seemingly opposite views.

"God wants us to take care of ourselves and be good to ourselves the same way we would be good to a best friend, doesn't he?" some folks suggest. "How can we ever love someone else if we don't have a healthy love for ourselves?"

Others, though, have a different take on the matter. "Doesn't Jesus want us to deny ourselves for the sake of him and others?" these people ask. "What else could he mean when he tells us to take up our crosses and follow him?"

Two such contrasting sentiments! Yet haven't most of us heard both of them, if we poll enough people in our faith communities and among our other friends? What is going on here? Psychologically, the first response makes intuitive sense. Yet biblically, how do we deal with the second?

Teachings that some of us have received from church only add to the confusion. One friend shared with me that she had been taught in Sunday school to have three priorities when it came to loving. First, she was meant to love Jesus; second, she was meant to love others; and third, almost as an afterthought, she was meant to love herself. Well, that sounded very pious! But it didn't take her long to realize that given those guidelines, if the people she was trying to love cared nothing about her in return, she would end up burned out and depleted, with no one, humanly speaking, looking out for her at all!

That couldn't be what Jesus would want, my friend finally decided. After all, the very wording of the second great commandment—"love your neighbor as yourself"—presupposes healthy self-love as a standard of comparison. So, there we are, brought right back to the same question with which we started. In what way does God want us to love ourselves?

SELF-LOVE AND GOD'S LOVE FOR US

What we need to remember here is the beautiful verse in 1 John 4:19, "We love because he first loved us." True, in the context of that passage John is speaking primarily of our love for one another, but surely the phrase "love your neighbor as yourself" implies that self-love should be included as well. God must want us to know how much he loves us and to draw on that knowledge for inspiration as we anchor our love for ourselves and others in a trusting relationship with the Lord. How can we gain a healthy self-acceptance or become the complete men and women God wants us to become without finding our essential identity in relationship with the One who created, sustains, and lovingly guides us? Doesn't the realization that we are deeply loved by God give us our bedrock for spiritual and personal growth? As another friend said to me just the other day, "If you don't think God loves you, how can you ever love yourself?"

The problem, of course, is that it is one thing to tell ourselves that God loves us and quite a different thing to feel this in our hearts. Just think about it a minute. Haven't a lot of us heard folks say almost sheepishly over the years, "Sometimes I can hardly believe God could really love me, given all the things that I know about myself!" Perhaps we have even thought that about ourselves.

For people who grew up in abusive or rejecting families and carry deep wounds as a result, believing that God loves them can indeed feel almost impossible. But even those of us who grew up in relatively normal homes may sometimes find doubts about God's love for us creeping into our hearts.

Such doubts reveal a huge misunderstanding, of course, since Scripture testifies that God's love is based entirely on grace and is not dependent on what we do or do not do from our own human end; it has nothing to do with our "deserving" it. One of my favorite books about God's unconditional love is *What's So Amazing About Grace?* by Philip Yancey. Despite our instinctive sense that we must somehow *earn* God's love, Yancey stresses that there is really nothing we can do—either good or bad—that will change God's constant and deep love for us.[1]

This does not mean, of course, that God is content for us to remain bound by whatever sins happen to be entangling us. It is precisely *because* God loves us so much that he also wants to challenge us to transcend areas of sin in our lives and to become the best that we can be. The Lord wants us to turn away from—that is, to "deny"—destructive attitudes and behaviors which may be enslaving us, so we will be better able to love both ourselves and others in good and fruitful ways. C. S. Lewis makes exactly this point in *Mere Christianity*, emphasizing that it is God's deep love for us that makes God so determined we should be cured of our sins.[2]

As our belief deepens that God loves us and wants the best for us— as we begin to believe this in our hearts as well as in our minds, I mean—we will be more likely to want to live according to our understanding of God's will for our lives. We will care to draw on the gifts God has given us and the joy that exercising those gifts can bring both to us and to others; we will want to transcend personal areas of sin so that we can grow into the full women and men that God created us to be; we will long to discover and develop our essential identity in Christ. To desire this and to take steps toward

---

1. Yancey, *What's so Amazing About Grace?*, 71.
2. Lewis, *Mere Christianity*, 133.

it is surely one important aspect of what it means to love ourselves in a truly biblical fashion.

I doubt it will surprise anyone that I am about to suggest that the journey into neighbor-love can provide a wonderful context for pursuing just this kind of growth! First, though, I want to take a little detour, as it were. It is important to recognize that there are times in all our lives when we need to be replenished and restored by experiencing God's love for us in fresh new ways, before focusing on outreach to our neighbors. Just this morning, as I type this, an email popped up in my Inbox which described a retreat aimed at folks living lives of Christian service who need time apart from immersion in others' needs so as to rest more deeply in God's love for *them*.

To acknowledge our common need for this sort of periodic restoration is also a crucial aspect of biblical self-love. For this reason, I want to mention one special resource here. I am thinking about retreats sponsored by the Cursillo Movement that are specifically designed to offer participants an experiential encounter with the love of God. Cursillo retreats are widely available for both men and women in Episcopal and Roman Catholic churches, as well as in other denominations like The United Methodist Church, where they are called "Walk to Emmaus" retreats. So, what are these retreats like?

EXPERIENCING GOD'S LOVE
THROUGH CURSILLO

Wanting to hear a first-hand description of how these retreats nurture a deeper awareness of God's love and a deeper sense of identity in Christ, I decided to call my friend John, who has been involved with Cursillo for a number of years now, initially making his retreat out in Seattle as a way of supporting his wife Sandy in *Kairos*, her Cursillo sponsored prison ministry. As it turned out, that retreat was transformative for him.

It all began on the Thursday night he arrived at the church, uncertain what to expect. Right away leaders set the tone for the next three days by asking participants to relinquish watches and pagers (now, John laughs, it would be cell phones!), to be sure that there would be no interruptions from the outside world and to allow for total immersion in the retreat's focus on God and God's love.

Over the course of the weekend, members of the Cursillo team delivered thirteen talks on faith, hope, and love. The days built in spiritual and emotional intensity until Saturday night when, after a beautiful dinner, participants were led, singing, to another building, ostensibly to thank the kitchen staff for the meal they had just enjoyed. What they found when they arrived, however, was a magnificent surprise, so awe-inspiring that John decided we should not describe it here, lest foreknowledge dampen the joy of the experience for potential Cursillo retreatants who might be reading this!

Suffice it to say that throughout the weekend, ministry leaders showed such loving attention to detail that a hundred grace-filled moments became for participants moving embodiments of God's love. On Sunday morning everyone celebrated their "new birthday," the start of their "new life in Christ," and when family members gathered on Sunday afternoon to hear retreatants describe what the three days had meant to them, there were many tears of joy.

In fact, John marveled, the whole weekend was a tear-filled time. He was taken by surprise at the depth of emotion he and others felt; he had not been expecting that. One thing that really struck him was his longing for others in his family to experience God's love as he himself had been experiencing it during the retreat. Sharing what it had felt like, John recalled Alastair Sim's portrayal of Scrooge in the 1951 version of "A Christmas Carol," and Scrooge's tears of joy after he was given his second chance. For John, that expressed it completely.

Did that deep experience of God's love last afterwards? I wanted to know. John acknowledged that obviously, returning to ordinary life after something like that is bound to feel like coming down from the mountaintop back into the valley. Recognizing this, Cursillo offers "Fourth Day" groups for graduating retreatants who want to keep the experience alive and to build on it for future growth. Members are invited to continue in these ongoing fellowship groups for the rest of their lives, and this John has been doing.

Describing his own group experience, John explained that conversation focuses on three topics: first, "close moments" with God that members have experienced over the past week; second, what they are currently studying that is helping them better understand God's love; and third, what action—"apostolic action"—they are taking in their lives to share God's love with others. Regarding that last theme, John's Seattle group jointly sponsored a child in Sierra Leone through "Children of the Nations." In addition to this, men had individual ministries in the community. One worked with a local food bank. Another mentored folks at a halfway house for recovering addicts. John himself served behind the scenes at the prison where his wife Sandy had her *Kairos* ministry, scrubbing pots and pans and preparing food for the inmates.

John was not only a faithful member of Seattle's Fourth Day group for the duration of his and Sandy's stay on the west coast. When they moved to New Hampshire a few years ago, he established and currently leads an ongoing group in the church they joined there. He also stays in touch with friends in Seattle's Fourth Day group, for relationships forged in Cursillo through the power of the Holy Spirit remain deeply and permanently blessed.

How has John's involvement with Cursillo changed him over the years? I wanted to know. His response to that question was eloquent. It has given him a passion to pursue Bible study more deeply, he explained, and to share his love of the Bible and of Jesus with others. The Fourth Day group is a hugely important resource, for the depth of trust and personal sharing that participants experience together is very hard for most men to come by in the world at large. Group members really grow to care about each other and about each other's lives. And of course, the love among members of this neighborly community helps everyone continue to experience God's love more fully and, as a consequence, to love God, their neighbors, and themselves more deeply in return. Once again, there is that same theme . . . love of neighbor, love of the Lord, and love of oneself. How intertwined they all are!

SELF-EXPLORATION AS WE SEEK
TO LOVE OUR NEIGHBORS

So, retreats like Cursillo can be a key resource for those seeking replenishment in their awareness of God's love for *them*. Similarly, books exploring the topic of spiritual formation frequently offer guidance on how contemplative prayer and other spiritual disciplines can help people connect with God's love in their depths. One wonderful example, which I mentioned previously, is Henri Nouwen's *Spiritual Formation: Following the Movements of the Spirit*. Another helpful title that reflects increasing usage of these disciplines in evangelical protestant churches is Ruth Haley Barton's *Sacred Rhythms: Arranging Our Lives for Spiritual Transformation*.

This whole subject of spiritual disciplines and contemplative prayer is so rich that really to address it would be to begin an entirely new book, one which I am certainly not qualified to write! The mystery of how we discover our place in God's loving heart as we move more deeply into our own is just that—a mystery. Because I feel so inadequate to speak of these matters out of my own experience, and because this book is offering *beginning* reflections on a spirituality of service, I will not try to delve further into this rich and vast area right now. What I will do is simply to mention one basic insight frequently voiced by Elizabeth O'Connor and others: namely, that any inward journey into our own depths remains incomplete if it does not point us back to an outward journey into relationship with our neighbors—and vice versa. This basic principle undergirds Church of the Saviour's entire spiritual philosophy and is spelled out particularly well in *Journey Inward, Journey Outward*.[3]

To underline and elaborate on O'Connor's point about the interrelationship of the inward and outward journeys, I just want to suggest that some of us may actually find inner reflection to be most helpful when God gives us the resource of new *outer* experiences on which we can reflect! Relationships that unfold when we reach out to our neighbors can provide just this kind of resource; they can give us a wealth of experiential material to ponder as we identify important questions to bring to God in prayer.

3. O'Connor, *Journey Inward, Journey Outward*, 28–30.

When we reach out to become more compassionately involved in others' lives, we discover a great deal about who we really are. Some of our encounters may reveal an empathy and concern we did not realize we had, but honest reflection on other encounters will surely put us in touch with our limitations—defensiveness and judgmentalism, perhaps; or areas in which we find it hard to forgive and to receive forgiveness; or ways that we have failed to understand who we really are in God.

Sincere prayer that grows out of reflection on our encounters with others is bound to draw us closer to the Lord, for prayer that is motivated by the desire to love our neighbors more fruitfully is surely prayer which God will honor and in which God will lovingly meet us. Then, as we ask questions sparked by our desire to love in more helpful ways, we may find ourselves embarked on a rich inner journey, a transforming encounter both with God and with ourselves.

What are our real gifts? How does Jesus truly want us to follow him? How are we called to balance self-development against involvement with others? What weaknesses and sins do we need to work on in order to become more creative people for others and for ourselves? How do we need to be healed in our own depths to be more fruitful members of God's kingdom? What about our own relationship with God? Where are we trusting and where resisting? These are just some of the questions we may find ourselves exploring as we reach for the capacity to become the loving people God desires us to be.

Anyone curious about how rich this kind of self-reflection can be might want to look at *The Road to Daybreak: A Spiritual Journey*, Henri Nouwen's intimate journal covering the year beginning with the summer of 1985, after he resigned his teaching position at the Harvard Divinity School, till the time he began his new position in August of 1986 as priest to the intellectually handicapped residents and their assistants at L'Arche Daybreak in Canada, one of the world-wide L'Arche communities in which mentally challenged individuals and so-called "normal" people live together and share their lives. In this journal Nouwen reveals both his hard struggles and his faithful commitment to following Jesus as he made his way against steep resistance and anxiety toward this new way of serving the Lord, a mode of service that was frighteningly at odds with his academic life up until that point.

Most of us will probably not be dealing with the sort of radical faith journey Nouwen's journal reveals and the vulnerabilities it exposes. Still, when we seek to explore questions that our own experiences of neighbor-love raise for us, we can face uncomfortable challenges. We may want the support of our pastors along the way, or of discerning and trustworthy Christian friends. Or we might want to seek out a spiritual director with special skills to guide us on the journey.

Because this kind of inner exploration may sound threatening to some, or perhaps too "self-involved," it is important to stress that we are really talking about *prayer* here, about reflective conversation with God and with ourselves, through the ministry of the Holy Spirit; we are not talking about mere introspection. The distinction is crucial. In *The Healing Presence* Leanne Payne cautions readers to avoid what she calls "the disease of introspection" in which we can become trapped and closed in on ourselves. She urges people always to look to God, seeking what the Lord wants to show them as they search their own hearts.[4] In a related vein, Elizabeth O'Connor stresses in *Journey Inward, Journey Outward* that a full and fruitful journey inward will always involve *engagement with God* and *engagement with others* as well as *engagement with oneself*.[5]

When these three dimensions are present and interconnected, then the self we discover through prayerful reflection will increasingly reveal our essential identity in the Lord. As this happens, we will be better able to love God and our neighbors in the ways most suited to us, which in turn will continue to nurture our true identity in Christ. Finally,—and once again—caring to develop this identity in Christ must be one important aspect of what it means to love ourselves in the way that God intends.

4. Payne, *The Healing Presence*, 164.

5. O'Connor, *Journey Inward, Journey Outward*, 10–27.

A PRISON MINISTRY NURTURES
A DEEPER IDENTITY

Sometimes lay ministries in which we are involved can help us discover and develop multi-faceted aspects of who we are in God. Just the other day my friend Elise, my one-time supervisor at the library (and co-driver for Willard!), was reminiscing with me about her own experience with such a journey in the context of a jail ministry she and her husband had joined together a number of years ago. This ministry was called REC—"Residents Encounter Christ."

REC has its roots in Cursillo, the movement described a few pages back that sponsored John's transformative retreat. The purpose of REC is to bring something of the Cursillo experience to people in jail, offering them during a three-day weekend an opportunity to encounter Christ and the kind of loving community the Holy Spirit creates. On a REC weekend members of the ministry team, who have previously met together for several months of prayer and planning, come into the jail to share their lives and their stories with the residents there. Prior to that, though, they must go through a period of preparation: searching their own hearts and reflecting on their own experiences as they formulate the insights and testimonies they will be sharing with the residents assigned to them.

"What we really did there," Elise reminisced, "was to trust these people with our most intimate selves, our most intimate experiences. We told them how we met Jesus. We shared mistakes we had made, sins we had fallen into, all the dark broken areas of our lives. You know, in a way this was taking an awful chance, to be so trusting. But everyone has a story, after all; everyone has pain. And who would understand pain better than these people in prison?

"Anyway, what happened was that they took our pain. They received it, and in doing so, something very healing came around. We all got this tremendous experience of love and community. We really bonded together in spirit, soul, mind, and heart with these men. And it was all through the power of the Holy Spirit guiding us and orchestrating the whole weekend, even down to details like the order in which our talks were given."

"What exactly did all this mean for you?" I wanted to know.

Elise thought for a long moment. Then she finally replied, "You know, the most intimate talk I ever gave on REC weekends—one that I repeated five or six times, actually, because it always seemed to carry so much power—had to do with an area of sin in my life that I was always very reluctant to share with people in general, but that somehow God enabled me to share with these men. And you know, each time I told this story, another part of me was healed. What happened was that through all the different people who heard my pain and received it, each time something else in me was touched. But you know," and suddenly she laughed, "Jesus always left just enough repentance in me each time so that my grief was still alive the next time I shared with the next group of people!"

"Are there other ways REC helped you to find a deeper identity in Christ?" I asked.

"Well," Elise mused, "it affected my identity as a Christian very deeply, changed the whole way I come to God in prayer. I always find that when I bring the message of Jesus' unconditional love to someone else, I learn an enormous amount about his love for me at the same time. We all have this feeling deep down inside, I think—you know, this sense of, 'How could Jesus possibly really love me, knowing all these terrible secrets I carry around in my heart?' But somehow when I experienced his love there among the REC team, and the love we were giving and receiving with the residents . . . Well, God's love for me just became believable in a whole new way.

"Then too, I discovered a lot about who I am as a Christian woman. I mean, I realized that a woman really does bring something special to this sort of ministry that a man can't bring. There's a nurturing, a gentleness in caring . . . And living this out, being there as other people were living it out, I could see that a woman can touch a part of these men that hasn't been touched by sensitive nurturing in so many years, maybe never. The residents saw those of us who were married, with our husbands; and even the single women, they came to see them differently too, as real sisters in Christ. I think that all of us women on the team came to experience ourselves more deeply as the women God created us to be. I know that I did.

"Then finally, REC brought Scripture to life for me in a whole new way. There are two passages of Scripture that never meant anything to me personally before; they were just words. One is the passage in Matthew 25:35–36, 'For I was hungry and you gave me something to eat, I was thirsty and you gave me something to drink . . . I was in prison and you came to visit me.' That last line, especially, has really come alive for me. Now every time I hear those words read, I really get emotional, because now I know what this kind of sharing can mean to someone on the inside, someone who's felt abandoned, someone who's felt like they were nothing . . . And then the other passage that means so much to me now is the first verse in Matthew 7, 'Do not judge, or you too will be judged.' That has become very, very powerful."

As our conversation was drawing to a close, Elise added one last thought. "You know," she said, "there's a saying in the ministry that goes something like this: 'God doesn't care what we have been. He only cares about what we can now become—in him.'"

What we can now become—in him. That is a beautiful invitation. Obviously, experiences like Elise's in REC do not mean that we will never again struggle as our lives unfold. But even if we do, foundational strengths we have gained through closeness to God in relationships of neighbor-love will still be there in our spirits and in memory for us to draw on over time, as we continue to develop a deeper identity in the Lord.

Elise's journey with REC brought her to a better understanding of her identity in so many ways: through the healing of painful memories as she shared them with residents in the jail and saw those residents being helped by her words; by experiencing God's unconditional love for herself more deeply as she described his unconditional love to those men; by coming to a new understanding of herself and her special capacity to love as a Christian woman; and finally, by discovering a richer relationship with Scripture as verses came to life for her in new ways, based on her experiences in REC.

RELINQUISHING FALSE SELF-IMAGES

So, in some cases particular experiences of neighbor-love can bring us quite dramatically to a deeper awareness of who we are in God, the way Elise's jail ministry did for her. Sometimes, though, it may take a while before we discern the path God wants us to follow. For any number of reasons, we may be blocked for a time when it comes to seeing where God really wants us. Yet even so, if we continue to search for God's guidance, eventually God will surely show us what we need to know. He will bring us to the place where our blinders fall away, our false self-images dissolve, and at last we will be able to see where we truly belong. Sometimes what we need to relinquish to reach this point may be as basic as our own self-consciousness and pride. For at times we may take our own "discipleship agendas" so seriously that we end up focusing more on ourselves than on the God who has been patiently waiting to help us—if only we would ask!

Once I had an eye-opener of a lesson in this respect. At the time of separation so many decades ago, as I waited for my divorce to become final, I used to spend hours huddled on the daybed in the tiny Cambridge apartment I was subletting, reading and re-reading Elizabeth O'Connor's books about Washington, DC's Church of the Saviour. I was at my most broken, isolated, and terrified, and as I lay there, this church came to life through Elizabeth O'Connor's words and became for me a precious beacon of hope. What a rich new life I might have, I used to fantasize, if only I could be part of this community! Surely (I told myself), if I lived down there I could re-discover all the meaning and sense of self-worth that divorce had stripped from me.

Could I go down to Washington right then? How I longed to do so! But even in my state of emotional confusion, I was wise enough to realize I was too needy to make such a move at that time. So, I found a library job back in western Massachusetts, bought a little house, and began attending College Church, where eventually I became involved in setting up and volunteering at our emergency shelter. As I described earlier in this book, working there in the shelter was a marvelous gift. Still, despite the reality of all the blessings I experienced there, my fantasy of belonging to Church of the Saviour continued to haunt me for several more years. Then, finally, the glimmerings of an idea began to take shape in my mind . . .

Yes, I had been too needy to move to Washington right after divorce, I acknowledged to myself. But was it possible that at long last I might finally be mature enough to take this step? Certainly, I was a lot stronger at that point, spiritually and psychologically.

Looking around my little house that spring, I felt an almost irresistible urge to sever all ties with Northampton, pick up stakes, and make the move on the spot. Somehow, though, I had no peace about doing this. Then one day, after a time of prayer and journaling, a clear thought surfaced in my mind.

"You could just find a room in someone's house and rent it for a year," I told myself. "Go down once or twice a month, for three or four days each trip. Try it out. Volunteer at one of the missions of Church of the Saviour. Attend services. Get to know the people there. See how that feels and whether the wish to join this church deepens or fades."

So that is exactly what I did, and it turned out to be a very important time. Some of what I saw about myself was just too obvious for me to ignore the implications.

What did it mean, for instance, that I spent so much more time exploring Maryland condos and tiny townhouses in Virginia than I did checking out ministries of Church of the Saviour? Granted, I would need a place to live if I were to move, but surely tracking down real estate ought not to be the main purpose of these trips! It was certainly beginning to look as though full-time service in DC's inner city was not the biggest dream in my heart.

For that matter, what did it mean that I spent so much time in Alexandria where a dear friend from high school now lived, walking the banks of the Potomac with her, playing with her children, sharing long talks with her over cappuccino in Olde Towne coffee houses? When I went into the Adams-Morgan section of Washington, where most of Church of the Saviour's ministries were located, I found myself clutching my purse tighter to me. Those dubious looking folks hanging out by the abandoned movie theater were,

I suspected, drug dealers, and they filled me with fear. I was only too conscious of a prayer I had been startled to find in the printed bulletin at one of the church's worship services. "Lord," it had read, "Help us to forgive those of our neighbors who have assaulted us."

Eventually I faced the truth. The way my longing for Church of the Saviour membership seemed to fade in the light of reality-testing could only mean one thing: I was not really called to move to Washington at all. It had been a fantasy of my own, a false self-image, and never God's plan.

One morning I awoke in my rented Arlington bedroom feeling badly depressed. I tried to pray but couldn't. My thoughts were floating aimlessly, dismally; my mind refused to focus on God.

Who was I really in Christ, if not "a Church of the Saviour person"? And why had this self-image grabbed hold of me so tenaciously? What loneliness or insecurity was making me try so desperately to define myself in this fashion?

I still didn't know. But then, at precisely that instant, an entirely different insight crystallized in my mind. This realization that my dreams for a Washington move were based on a false self-image had taken *me* by surprise. But surely this was far from a new revelation to God! Hadn't God always known the deepest truths of my heart and even foreseen where I would be on this particular morning? None of my early experiences of God's love could be in any way invalidated by this new development. That love was then, and remained now, unconditional and all accepting, encompassing in advance my present discouragement, redeeming and transforming it with an infinite grace.

Oh, could this really be true? Could it really be that God loved and accepted me just as I was and that there was no need for me to become a radically surrendered Christian who wore, as my seal of approval, a metaphorical badge stamped "Church of the Saviour member"? My mind understood that indeed this was so, but my heart could scarcely believe it. Could it be that my fears of accepting who I really was were based on a huge misconception? Could God simply have been waiting patiently all these years for the moment when I could face myself and thus come to him, with all my fantasies and false self-images collapsed around me?

I had not felt able to pray at first as I lay there that dismal Arlington morning, but as all these insights unfolded, I started to suspect I had been praying more than I knew. Gradually then, in the days that followed, I began to understand many things I had scarcely allowed myself to see before, so blinded had I been by notions of who I myself had decided that I needed to be.

Many things were unfolding in Northampton. One reason I didn't get down to Washington as often as I had intended was that while I had planned to back away from my College Church shelter involvement that year, actually I had got drawn in more deeply in spite of myself. We had expanded to include a much larger supper program in addition to sleeping facilities; the number of our guests was growing; volunteer recruiting and scheduling were taking more time. In fact, a great deal of what Washington had symbolized to me was actually happening right there back home in Massachusetts. We had not yet formed our oversight committee which was soon to become a College Church variation on the theme of Church of the Saviour's mission groups. Still, our program, and hence my involvement with it, was growing. But at a pace—and in a place—more suited to my personality. It was happening according to God's timing, God's plan, and not according to idealized agendas of my own.

Moreover, if my Washington experiment had not led me closer to Church of the Saviour, it had proved crucial in a number of other ways. Evelyn, from whom I was renting my room, was a writer. At breakfast that year, at supper, over coffee, she and I spent hours sharing ideas, looking over her poems and essays, discussing my own visions for possible writing that someday I might do. We became good friends, and in the process, I found that this important component of my own identity—the component of "writer"—was being graciously reinforced.

God, I gradually realized, did not want me to move down to Washington, DC at all. God wanted me exactly where he had placed me, in Northampton, Massachusetts. But God did want me to have that rich, revealing year, whose insights I had so fought accepting.

What did I come to understand through this experience? The gospel mandates—to feed the hungry; to clothe the naked; to visit the sick—were still there. But God, I was beginning to see, wanted me—as he surely wants us all—to respond to this challenge in a way consistent with the personality I had been given. For each of us there is a way of living that will draw out our God given interests, gifts, and capacities at the same time that it challenges and disciplines us at the point of the gospel's call. When we learn to live in this fashion and take steps to do so, we will quite literally be learning how to love our neighbors as ourselves.

Is it as hard for others to realize this as it seems to have been for me? The notion that God could love and accept me as who I am, without wanting to turn me into someone else; the thought that the unique design of my individuality has been coded into my being and is precious in God's eyes; the idea that the authentic gifts God has planted in me need never be permanently renounced, but will turn out to be the raw materials he will use to bring me to my deepest and most complete identity in him—all of this sometimes seems too good to be true, too glorious to comprehend.

Why is it so hard really to believe this? Yes, God asks us to exercise self-denial at times, to take up our crosses and follow him. But this will not be in order to demolish the dreams, gifts, and yearnings that constitute our true selves. Rather, it will be to prune us and shape us, so that after we have learned some basic lessons in faithful living, God can give those dreams back to us again and help us bring them to fruition—not merely for our private self-fulfillment, but for the sake of God's unfolding kingdom. As this happens, we will finally be learning how to love our neighbors as ourselves. We will be growing into the women and men God designed us to be; we will be loving God and experiencing authentic biblical self-love as we embrace our true identity in the Lord.

REFLECTIVE QUESTIONS: CHAPTER 4

1. In general, are you able to feel in your heart that God loves you, or is it hard for you to believe this? If your ability to feel this ebbs and flows, can you identify causes for this variation? If you cannot really believe that God loves you, have you ever

taken your doubts to a pastor or spiritual counselor? If not, would you want to consider doing so?

2. If you have indeed experienced God's love for you, what has most communicated this awareness to you? A biblical verse? The compassion of a friend or loved one? A worship service? An experience in prayer? Choose and pray over a passage of Scripture that best conveys for you God's unchanging faithfulness and love.

3. What does the word "introspection" mean to you? If your attempts at self-examination have involved a sense of being closed in on yourself, make a conscious effort the next time you are engaging in self-reflection to look up to God and out of yourself. Ask God to reveal to you any truths about yourself that he wants you to understand, as well as their implications for how you might be a more loving person for others. Record in your journal any insights that you receive.

4. What ways of serving or being with others have energized you most in the past? If you let yourself daydream about various ministry possibilities, which dreams make you feel you are "coming to life" in a fresh way? Read Psalm 37:4 and ask the Lord to help you discern the desires he himself has planted in your heart, which he wants to bring to fruition.

5. What dreams or ambitions are presently bound up with your self-image? Have you experienced blocks when it comes to living out any of these that might indicate they are preventing you from discovering your true self in God? What does it feel like to contemplate relinquishing your hold on any ambitions or idealized goals that repeatedly "don't work" for you? Ask God to guide you and help you where this is concerned.

Chapter 5

Selfhood and Relationships

Over the past few years several local church communities have been involved in helping refugee families to resettle here in Northampton through their "Circles of Care," clusters of concerned folk committed to welcoming and coming around these families as they begin to build their new lives. College Church's Circle of Care has been active in supporting one of these families, as has the Circle of Care at St. John's Episcopal Church. Recently a friend from St. John's was describing to me the extraordinary experience that he and others have had, participating in this program. Sharing this story, he introduced me to a word I had not heard before, the African word *ubuntu*. This refers to the philosophical concept that one's sense of self is shaped by one's relationship with others. "I am because we are" is a proverbial sentence often quoted to express its essential meaning.

"I AM BECAUSE WE ARE"

My friend Judson marveled at how this concept of *ubuntu* became real in an amazing way to the group of parishioners at St. John's who embraced responsibility for helping the family assigned to them. This family—Maombi, her husband Albert, and their toddler Wilson—had recently arrived in the states from a refugee camp in Rwanda when Judson and a small group of others drove down to the Hartford airport on a cold, rainy April night three years ago as of this writing, to pick them up and bring them to Northampton.

They embodied sheer exhaustion, Judson recalled, with little Wilson looking like nothing but a bundle wrapped in bright cloth, strapped onto his mother's back! But providentially, resources for the family's needs began falling into place almost immediately as soon as they arrived: a single-family house was offered for free; people outside the parish came aboard to pitch in with grocery shopping, referrals to doctors and dentists, assistance with money management, furnishings, job referrals, rides whenever transportation was needed, and—especially—babysitting. People flocked forward to help. And before the family moved from Northampton to rejoin relatives who had preceded them to the states and been resettled in Utah, another baby had been born at Northampton's Cooley Dickinson Hospital, and the pediatrician who had joined the Circle after her first babysitting gig was instrumental in ensuring that the birth and the after-care went beautifully.

The entire experience was a huge gift for those in the Circle of Care. It didn't take long before the deeper meaning behind that concept of *ubuntu*—"I am because we are"—became a living reality to all concerned, for the folks who were helping realized almost immediately that they themselves were the true recipients of grace, as this extraordinary family welcomed them in amazing ways. "*Murakawa neza* in Kinyarwandan or *Karibu* in Swahili— 'Welcome!'—rang out every time you knocked on their door," said Judson. Little Wilson became the "outreach coordinator." People fell in love with this toddler as he beckoned everyone to come into his family's life with such endearing gestures, pointing to his parents and holding out his tiny arms in open-hearted invitation.

"It wasn't just little Wilson, though," Judson was quick to point out. "Of course, we all loved him immediately. But we couldn't get over how the entire family was so trusting. Maombi always radiated this powerful faith, hope, gratitude, and hospitality. Given everything they had been through, this trust they extended to us became a huge gift. Pretty soon everything got turned around. Each of us in the Circle, when we thought of the family, no longer found ourselves wondering, 'What can I do for you?' but instead marveling,

'How good it is to have you in my life!'" That proverbial sentence expressed by the word *ubuntu*—"I am because we are"—was no longer an abstraction but was now something to be tasted and known.

LOVING OTHERS, SELF-LOVE, AND CODEPENDENCY

A number of years ago another friend and I attended a lecture whose topic was an intriguing variation on this theme. The lecture was delivered by the late theologian and poet Dom Sebastian Moore; "Toward a Psychology of Self-Love," it was titled. In this talk Moore was examining self-love in a different way from the way that the concept is often understood; he was exploring how we come to know and appreciate ourselves more fully—to love ourselves more completely—when we experience ourselves as being enriched by deep caring for another.

True self-love, Moore suggested that afternoon, is not love *for* the self, in the sense of focusing on or cherishing one's own personality. Rather, it is a caring that proceeds *out of* the self, called into being by another, reaching out into the world as longing and desire, until the yearning to enrich the life of this other person awakens us to a new depth of being, a new awareness of our own significance.

My friend had a question after Sebastian Moore's lecture that afternoon. "But what happens to my sense of self if the one I love doesn't value my caring?" she wanted to know. "If I dare really to love someone else, and they don't love me in return, won't I then actually be losing myself instead of finding myself more deeply?"

It is a significant question, especially when it comes from someone who has been abandoned in previous relationships. Indeed, when we have been wounded in this way it may be crucial to keep boundaries particularly sturdy for a while in order to rebuild our strength. At such times we need to respect our frailty and to protect ourselves from excessive vulnerability.

Yet if we are ever going to venture into genuine love relationships, the plain truth is that we cannot do so without risking some vulnerability. In *The Four Loves* C. S. Lewis warns readers that the only way we can be certain of keeping our heart intact is to withhold our love from everyone around us. If we insist on protecting ourselves like this indefinitely, though, the terrible price we will pay is that our heart will simply die spiritually inside of us.[1]

God after all, designed us to be in redemptive relationships with one another. God calls us to love and empathy and sharing; the Lord invites us to break out of prisons of isolation and to be woven into ever new patterns of interconnection, in which others' concerns truly become our own. Whatever strengths we have managed to build into our identity and whatever gifts we have developed—all are enriched exponentially when we open ourselves to deep and prayerful involvement with the people God brings into our lives.

Yet if God is calling us to risk and to be vulnerable, this is not a call to "risk" as "the world" understands it. The distinction is crucial; to articulate it is to begin to address the concern behind my friend's question.

"Worldly" anxiety fears that we may not "get" the husband, the wife, the friend, whom we feel we need to complete our identity; it fears that we may not "get" enough attention, or love, or praise. Within such a perspective, rejection does indeed threaten our very sense of self.

If we are centered in God, though, sustained by a love relationship with the Lord, then ultimately our security is not dependent on the response of another person. This frees us to care and to risk more deeply, for we know that however the other meets (or fails to meet) us, we will not be destroyed. Rooted in God, we can increasingly be free to love not primarily to "get" something in return, but simply because our deepening desire is to be a real source of caring and hope for the people God has placed on our hearts. Increasingly we can be free to care so much for another's growth and wellbeing that our concern for that other person enhances our awareness of who we truly are.

Already I can hear the skeptical voices, some of them coming from my own heart. "That's a lovely sentiment, a lovely ideal. But surely it is easier said than done." Yes, of course this is true. Indeed,

---

1. Lewis, *The Four Loves*, 169.

the irony is that it may be precisely those with an unhealthy "need to be needed," those with a tendency toward codependency, who find this vision most appealing and live it out in counterproductive ways. Even putting issues of codependency aside, anyone who has gone through the agony of watching a cherished relationship disintegrate may question whether the kind of love Sebastian Moore described in his lecture is ever really possible.

On our own strength alone, surely it is not. We need God's help. More concretely, we need to keep ourselves strong by living out our relationships in a biblical fashion that will allow those relationships to unfold as God intends. We need to submit our human loves to God, always keeping the Lord primary in our hearts, so that we do not rely excessively on our friends' and loved ones' responses to define our self-worth. We need to find our primary identity in our growing love relationship with the Lord.

Still, we are flesh and blood. We have human needs, and God knows this. We need practical help in following guidelines like this so that they do not remain flowery abstractions.

THE NEED FOR A CARING COMMUNITY

One of the best resources we can have here is membership in a community of caring and support where we will be able to trust in a general sense that if we are sick, or hungry, or lonely, others will be there for us. We need to be woven into a fabric of communal concern in which the principle of agape love is alive and operative.

Now paradoxically, in my experience, the best way to find this resource is to invest ourselves in the project of helping to create it for others. As a general rule, obedience to God's commands often reaps surprising rewards. In particular, the command to "do to others what you would have them do to you" (Matthew 7:12) turns out, when followed in our communal relationships, to yield rich fruit. If we practice offering agape love to those around us, we will be helping to create an environment in which we ourselves are more likely to receive such love in return.

Surely one of the best places to practice this kind of relational living is in our faith communities. There, after all, we have a wide range of people—a diverse cross-section of the body of Christ—with whom we can consciously cultivate relationships based on shared faith and grounded in intentional goodwill. If we approach our church relationships as contexts for helping to build this kind of loving Christian community for others, we will most likely begin to discover a neighborly community in which that agape love flows both ways. In the process, we may well find that we are focusing less on what relationships we happen to *have* (as though they were our possessions), and more on who we are *becoming*, in terms of our responses.

We may not have children of our own, for instance, but there will be many children in the congregation in whom we can invest ourselves. We may not happen to be married, but as we get to know the couples around us, we will be able to be supportive people to both men and women in our common faith journeys, and we can learn a great deal in the process. Clear adherence to biblical guidelines and rigorous honesty about our personal feelings will prevent any confusion, either on our part or on the part of others, about what such relationships mean. When fidelity is a bottom line commitment, and everyone knows beyond any shadow of doubt that the bonds of marital trust will not be violated, then a deep liberation occurs, and we are freed to care for one another in ways that would never be possible if we feared that our caring might be misunderstood. If we adopt what I like to think of as an eternal perspective, then limits that come with particular relationships—what is not and cannot be—simply stand as givens; we can accept these limits, because we are envisioning our ultimate spiritual fulfillment in an infinitely larger and richer eternal dimension. This allows us to be open to the many appropriate ways we *can* be with one another and encourage one another to grow into the people the Lord wants us to be, so that we can all make our most fruitful contributions together to God's unfolding kingdom.

It is important to emphasize that the point of such relationships is not to gather together with others who are exactly like ourselves so that we form a clique or coterie, as so often happens in secular life. Precisely because many or perhaps even most of our brothers and sisters in Christ may not be folks we would necessarily have chosen as special friends in the world at large, our bonding in God's family provides the opportunity—and the mandate—to practice caring for one another according to God's manner of caring, the way of agape love. Still, along the way we will surely discover some particular friendships in our faith communities in which common interests and temperamental compatibilities make for special joy.

SPECIAL FRIENDSHIPS IN SHARED MINISTRY

Church ministries—corporate projects of neighbor-love that a number of people share together—can be especially rich opportunities for developing friendships like this. I think of Lauren and Lynn, two women who came to know one another while volunteering at College Church's soup kitchen.

They had not known each other at the time they both signed up to work their first Monday night shift, and when they met that week they were both beginners, learning together. As it happened, they fell into warm conversation immediately, helping each other from scratch as they were both learning the ropes. From the start, Lauren marveled at how naturally Lynn seemed to share herself—and her faith—with the guests. How, Lauren wondered, could someone be that relaxed and comfortable, spontaneously opening herself up to others like that? At the very same time, as it turned out, Lynn was recognizing many gifts in Lauren! "I saw that first night," Lynn later shared, "how Lauren had gifts of mercy and service, even of administration, that could really be developed if she wanted to do that." And indeed, with Lynn's encouragement Lauren did soon become increasingly involved in the ministry.

Meanwhile, as they continued to share shifts in the soup kitchen, Lynn and Lauren were discovering an amazing number of parallel circumstances in their personal lives, parallel struggles they were both going through at the same time in which they could support and encourage each other. With each new discovery, their friendship deepened.

"It was an unlikely friendship in some ways," Lynn once reflected. "Our backgrounds were very different. But in other ways it was as if we were each handpicked by God to be there for the other. I really believe our friendship was ordained."

Lauren echoed this theme. "It was a godsend," she said. "To have a close friend who understood everything I was going through and who could bring the perspective of faith to that understanding and help me see ways that God might be working in my life to teach me some new lessons . . . Well, that was just very special. That was a unique resource."

Their friendship was also enriched by virtue of their belonging to a neighborly community together, through their joint ministry with the homeless. "We've been like a family," Lauren said once. "Just as it was so wonderful for Lynn and me to discover each other, it was also so wonderful for us both to discover so many similarities of soul with the men and women we were serving, beneath the superficial differences in social circumstances. It was all just so moving. And such a privilege. When someone says to you, 'Can I talk with you? I'm really hurting and I need someone to listen,' well, that's just an extraordinary feeling." What happened was that Lynn's and Lauren's friendship was nurtured by—and in turn helped to nurture—a widening experience of compassion in community.

This is exactly as it should be, for special friendships like this, set securely in the fabric of caring that ideally characterizes the body of Christ, provide the perfect context for our ongoing conversion into the women and men God calls us to become: for him; for others; and for ourselves. As we become ever more rooted in the Lord, ever more secure in the knowledge of who we are in his eyes, we will probably discover more and more opportunities for this kind of ongoing conversion.

DEEPER CONVERSION THROUGH
LOVING: A PERSONAL STORY

We may discover something else, as well. Occasionally, and quite unexpectedly, we may discover a new friendship in the most unlikely of places that calls forth from our hearts the special kind of caring that Sebastian Moore spoke of in his lecture—a caring in which our longing to enrich the life of another person awakens in us a new depth of being, a new awareness of our own significance. As this happens, we may feel a kind of glory breaking over us.

Now, if we see relationships as opportunities for ongoing conversion into the men and women God wants us to become, then this feeling of glory cannot go unchecked, nor can the relationship go unexamined. Quoting Jesus' stern words in Luke 14:26, C. S. Lewis reminds us of Christ's warning that we must never allow any human love to take precedence over our love for him, or to interfere with our willingness to follow where he leads us.[2]

When a love like the one Sebastian Moore described has ignited our hearts and collides with our first priority to seek and to follow Christ's call, this collision can drive us into a spiritual and emotional crucible. Quite unknowingly, I took my first steps toward such a crucible on a Sunday afternoon in mid-November many years ago—a couple of years, actually, after that revealing Washington sojourn had taught me that I belonged at College Church and not at Church of the Saviour.

It all started when I stumbled into an encounter whose ramifications I never could have predicted. One of our shelter guests had fallen ill at our program the night before, and a volunteer had taken him to the ER. The next day another volunteer on duty at the hospital's information desk had recognized his name and gone up to check on him. He could probably use some more visitors, she suggested to me later. Why didn't I go?

I wasn't especially eager to do so. I was very busy—what else was new?—and while I knew Matthew casually from the shelter and had seen him casually over the years around town or at the library, I had never felt any particular connection with him. But of course, I went. That day, as we sat together in the hospital solarium—a football game droned away on TV in the corner—there was space to talk on a different level. He began to share details of his life that

2. Lewis, *The Four Loves*, 171.

were new to me, and to talk about how it felt to live with his particular vantage point on the world.

It was an odd story he told, but as I sat there I was surprised to find myself suspending all critical judgment and simply listening. It was not so much the details I was absorbing, really, but rather his feelings, his world view, his whole inner landscape. And what I took in was this: his intense curiosity about the mysteries of reality; a marvelously clean detachment and dispassion toward himself even as he was also, quite obviously, carrying some complex troubles; a sort of debonair dignity; and a quirky, unique integrity, a personal code of honor. I absorbed all of this, reading between the lines of his narrative, and suddenly a thought caught fire in my mind. How much richer might Matthew's life feel, if only he could open himself to a relationship with God!

The ramifications were too huge, too complex, for me even to begin to put them into words. How I longed for the Holy Spirit to give me, right then and there, exactly the sentences Matthew needed to hear! It didn't happen, though. So, I remained silent, and the moment passed.

A couple of days later he was discharged from the hospital and came back to the shelter. We chatted; I inquired after his health. But in my heart, I could feel it gathering— the full weight of that unfinished conversation between us—and with that gathering, a deep, mounting sadness.

One morning after I had left the shelter from my overnight shift, and he had left with the other guests, I found myself driving aimlessly around, unable to return home. I was not on duty at the library that day and had nowhere I needed to be, as a bleak wind moaned and a monotonous rain beat steadily down. Finally, I headed back toward my house, turned into my driveway. But somehow, I couldn't go inside. So, I just sat there in the car while the rain streamed down over the windshield.

Beside me lay a copy of the Bible. I turned to one of my favorite psalms, Psalm 139, and began to read: *O Lord, you have searched me and you know me.* The words released something deep in my heart, and tears began to flow. I read further: *Where can I go from your Spirit? Where can I flee from your presence? If I go up to the heavens, you are there; if I make my bed in the depths, you are there.*

The words cleaved me, and my whole body shattered into sobs. And then, quite suddenly, it was as if God's own words were laid on my heart like a weight of pure gold: "This is the way I love Matthew Malone . . ." And then silence.

What do you do with an experience like that? What *can* you do? Nothing, at first—the emotion is too overwhelming. Finally, when you realize that you need to pray, you may not be able to do it alone.

And so, when I was at last able to collect myself sufficiently to leave the car and go inside, I found myself calling a friend from church who worked nearby.

The moment she heard my voice, her own was urgent with concern. "What's wrong? Something's happened, hasn't it? Are you all right? Do you want me to come over? I can leave on my break, I'm so close. I can come right now."

"No, no," I told her. "I'm all right, really. But I was just wondering if maybe . . . if maybe we could have lunch together in a little while. And maybe . . . pray together?"

"Of course," she told me instantly. "I can take an extended lunch hour. Come meet me at about eleven-thirty."

So, we had lunch together. But by then, of course, I couldn't talk about what had happened. So over salad, soup, and coffee, we skirted around the issue. Afterwards though, sitting in my friend's car before she had to go back to work, finally we prayed. She knew by then it was Matthew I wanted to pray for: I had got that much out.

"Whatever this is about," she told me, "you need to be the one who prays this one. I'll pray at the end, but the core of this prayer has to come from you." So there in her car, I prayed.

Usually I can remember every word I have spoken to God, but this time it was different. This time all memory of what I prayed was immediately lifted from me after the words were spoken. Simply erased. Whatever I said, though, it must have been deep. Because my friend was very moved.

Later that week in the privacy of my own heart, in the midst of another time of prayer, I said something else to God, and these words I do remember. "Lord," I prayed, "I don't understand any-thing about this, but one thing I do know. I need you to guide me here, to take whatever I am feeling and pattern it according to your will. *Give me your perfect love for Matthew. Your perfect love.*" Fi-nally, then, for the first time since the weight of that experience had descended on me, I knew peace.

In the wake of visiting Matthew in the hospital that day and finding my heart broken open by the power of God's deep love for him, suddenly I realized . . . that was God's love for *me*, as well! All my fears, all my resistance, all my need to be in control . . . God understood these failings, understood the reasons for them . . . *and loved me anyway.* Oh, what a glorious thought!

This realization, together with the longing that Matthew come to experience the grace of God's love, drew me into deeper and more sustained prayer than I had experienced in a long time. I found myself crying out to God to take me and use me in any way he might wish, if only I could be a helping influence in Matthew's life. Suddenly any inhibitions I had about fully yielding to the Lord seemed to have dissolved. None of my defensiveness mattered any longer. God was what mattered. God . . . And God's amazing love.

And, of course, Matthew. For—I need to say it clearly, lest what follows be compromised by my failure to have spoken the obvious truth—I had fallen in love with Matthew, even as I was, through that same experience, falling in love all over again with God.

As we became friends—very gradually and very tentatively—I knew I was walking a spiritual high wire. It was not really that I feared we would become sexually involved; deep down, somehow I knew that God would protect us from this. What I did fear was that my feelings might overwhelm me so powerfully that I would lose my capacity to be a helpful person in Matthew's life and—worse still—lose my capacity to remain anchored in the Lord.

That year I immersed myself in C. S. Lewis' *The Four Loves,* with its vision of how God can redeem and transform our imperfect human loves when we keep him first in our hearts and refuse to let natural loves become idolatrous. Falling in love, says Lewis, offers a special opportunity for spiritual conversion. This love transforms us so profoundly that suddenly one other person takes center stage for us in an extraordinary way, displacing our usual focus on our own concerns. If by God's amazing grace we were ever able to extend such self-giving love to the others around us, Lewis suggests, we would find we were fulfilling the command to love our neighbors as ourselves. Used rightly, he concludes, the gift of being in love can actually help us to grow in that direction.[3]

This vision became my touchstone that extraordinary year in the shelter, that extraordinary year my relationship with Matthew was unfolding. Time and again, day after day, I had to bring all my feelings to God in prayer. Time and again I wept out all the longing, confessed all the fear, pleaded with God from the depths of my soul for divine grace in this relationship, that I might transcend my own turbulence, remain available to play a creative role in the life of this man that I loved, and grow in my capacity to use the experience as Jesus wanted me to do.

How graciously God met me! For over time, as Matthew and I moved through several stages in our relationship—into real closeness for a while and then, over a somewhat bumpy path, into a more comfortably detached comradeship—I never lost the sense of God's mercy, compassion, and guidance.

Loving Matthew taught me as nothing else could, perhaps, that provided we are being faithful to God's standards, anchoring ourselves in our foundational commitment to the Lord, what will matter most in our human relationships will be the opportunity they provide to connect with God's love in our hearts. Somehow, by a gift of sheer grace, God enabled me to make just this kind of connection with him as Matthew and I grew to know one another more deeply.

BEYOND HUMAN INTIMACY: A DEEPER UNION WITH GOD

When our human relationships are increasingly anchored in our primary relationship with God, then indeed the particular course they take, naturally speaking, ultimately will matter less than our

3. Lewis, *The Four Loves*, 158.

inner assurance that we have lived them out according to God's will. For provided we have, we can leave the outcome in the Lord's hands, knowing that we have done everything possible from our human end to help them unfold in the best possible way. We may feel profound pain over what we see in our loved one's responses; it may seem, at times, that our hearts are being wrung from us. Still, at the deepest level of our being, deep down in our souls, we can pray that God will use our love for some eventual healing in an eternal perspective only God understands. This can be our comfort.

Finally, we can know for a certainty that (even in memory) it is God's presence in our obedient loving which ultimately abides. As we choose to open ourselves faithfully to those whom the Lord has placed on our hearts, we can simultaneously re-center ourselves in him—the One who never leaves us, the One in whose love we will always find our own true selves.

REFLECTIVE QUESTIONS: CHAPTER 5

1. What does the word "vulnerability" mean to you? Does it make you feel hopeful, or do you find it frightening? What have been your experiences with letting yourself be vulnerable in the past? If those experiences were hurtful, might a deeper dependence on Jesus, as your relational center, have helped you here? Does that concept feel like a possibility?

2. Read Acts 4:32–35. Admittedly, the extraordinary faith community described in this passage is not one we are likely to find duplicated today in our own churches. This said, do you feel that your local church embodies a godly spirit of mutual caring and concern? What steps might you yourself take to help build relationships in your church body that could better exemplify a spirit of genuine agape love?

3. In Chapter IV of *The Four Loves*, C. S. Lewis suggests that true Friendship is the least jealous of the loves, since when we share our friends, we each bring out different qualities in one

another, enriching the experience for all concerned.[4] Have you seen anything like this when friends share a common ministry together, interacting with their mutual "neighbors" in uniquely complementary ways? Share your impressions and memories with others.

4. In Acts 20:35 Paul quotes Jesus' words, "It is more blessed to give than to receive." Have you experienced the truth of this promise in your own life? In what kinds of contexts and in what kinds of ways do these words ring true to you, if at all?

5. Reflect on the fact that Christ calls us his "friends" if we do what he commands by loving one another to the point of death, as he has loved us (John 15:12–14). What do you make of this radically challenging thought? How do you relate to it?

---

4. Lewis, *The Four Loves*, 92.

Chapter 6

Selfhood and Surrender

Have you ever felt truly surrendered to God? Do you perhaps feel that now? Some of us may have lived through periods in our lives when we felt deeply surrendered to the Lord, only to find in the wake of those experiences that our commitment seemed to falter as the months wore on.

I remember one time shortly before I embarked on all those stressful years of commuting between Massachusetts and New Jersey to care for my elderly parents. Unexpectedly one day the whole left side of my body went mysteriously numb and remained like that for about three weeks. The only way I can describe this is to say that when I walked across the room, I felt as though I were clomping around on a block of ice! Doctors were unable to explain what was happening or to offer any treatment. Eventually the symptoms lifted on their own and never returned. The amazing thing is that during this whole time I was never crippled by worry over what was going on; instead I felt awe, even at times serenity, as I sensed God's protecting presence. My parents and I made many long distance phone calls back and forth while I was navigating this bizarre condition. I remember reassuring them more than once, "It's all right. *God knows what's happening to my body."* And I really meant it. As long as I knew that this was so—and in those moments I absolutely knew it—I was convinced that I needed nothing more. God's presence and love were sufficient. That felt like surrender indeed!

Another time when I felt fully surrendered was, of course, during that extraordinary year in the shelter when I fell in love with Matthew and threw myself totally on God's grace and guidance, begging the Lord to take me and use me in any way he wanted if I could just be a helpful influence in Matthew's life. During that whole period, I was intentionally and whole-heartedly asking God to take my life and use it, according to his will.

I just wrote "according to his will" . . . But of course, my real desire in this case was that God would use me in any way he wanted so as to fulfill my *own* will—namely, that I might be a blessing to Matthew. My prayer of surrender was genuine, yes; but it sprang from a very human love, not primarily from my love for God. And in the other example I just gave, the time I felt such radical trust in God and in God's protection during my mysterious illness, that abandoned faith was nothing I had asked for or chosen. The Holy Spirit had simply bestowed it on me as sheer gift. Such peace was alien to my natural anxiety-prone personality. And sure enough, as my symptoms lifted, my natural personality gradually reasserted itself.

Now, here is something very interesting. In the wake of that radical faith during my illness, I often found myself wondering whether God might have been giving me an invitation. "Now that you know what it feels like to abandon yourself to my love," I could imagine God might have been saying, "wouldn't you like to live this way from now on? You can open yourself unreservedly and let me show you a richer way of living than you can even begin to imagine. *You have that option.*"

Whether those were God's words or mine, their message remains true. All of us do indeed have the option of choosing to open ourselves to ever deeper levels of trust and surrender. But to contemplate surrendering this way with our own free will, with a sincere desire to live out God's vision for our lives rather than our own, is to face a real challenge. That prospect can feel daunting. At least, this is what I have often found in my own experience.

WHY DO WE FEAR SURRENDERING TO GOD?

Why are we afraid? To start with the most superficial reason, I have often wondered if there may not be something about the very word "surrender" that scares us. Think of all the connotations it has! When I asked one friend in church how that word struck her, she said, "You know, sometimes the word 'surrender' really does bother me. It sounds so military, doesn't it? I like 'yielding' much better." And a man whose entire life embodies what looks to me like true surrender, as he pours himself out unstintingly for God and for others, had this to say. "Well, I know that a lot of folks find the word 'surrender' inspiring, but to tell the truth, I never have. It sounds like we're quaking in our boots or something and saying to God, 'Okay, okay, I give up!' That's totally opposite to the sort of loving relationship I experience with the Lord in my own life."

Wow! That was pretty strong! It really does seem that the word "surrender" causes problems for some of us.

Looking back at some of my own struggles over the years, and reflecting on this question not too long ago, I decided to google the phrase "Bible verses about surrender," and up popped a link to "30 Powerful Bible Scriptures on Surrender." The choices were revealing, for when I looked them up, not a single one contained that actual word! Even more intriguing, many of them took me to verses I have always loved. Here is one of them, in Romans 12:2: "Do not conform any longer to the pattern of this world, but be transformed by the renewal of your mind." Those words have always inspired me; indeed, I have often consciously tried to live by them. If seeking to follow guidelines like this constitutes surrender, then maybe I was surrendering over the years more often than I knew at the time!

But I need to be honest here. Of course, it is not just the word "surrender" that has sometimes felt frightening. Let's face it; Jesus' own words can be scary as well. Take his warning in Luke 14:26: "If anyone comes to me and does not hate his father and mother, his wife and children, his brothers and sisters—yes, even his own life— he cannot be my disciple." Without going down the rabbit hole of trying to tease out just what Jesus means by that word "hate," it is enough to point out that this certainly presents a pretty radical challenge when it comes to ordering our relational priorities! Also, of course, we have that disturbing call in Matthew 10:38 where Jesus says, "and anyone who does not take his cross and follow me is not worthy of me."

This image of taking up one's cross can indeed be scary. In her book *The Healing Presence*, Leanne Payne acknowledges this, but suggests at the same time that when people are burdened with this kind of fear, it means that they have fallen under the sway of what she calls the "false self" that is separated from Christ. If instead one is walking in the Spirit, she continues, one can then know the joy of simply being open and available to hear and respond to God's call in our hearts. Any suffering that comes with this, she stresses, will be authentic and redemptive, far preferable to suffering that comes as a consequence of sin when we are separated from Christ. Offering her own definition of what it means to carry the cross, Payne shares that for her, it simply means "to practice the Presence of Jesus and allow His love to flow through us to others."[1]

"The Presence of Jesus" . . . If the word "surrender" carries disturbing connotations, this phrase "the Presence of Jesus" radiates promise. Indeed, even the frightening challenges that Jesus voices in the gospels can suddenly be transformed into gracious invitations. For instance, as we read through and beyond those words in Matthew 10:38—"anyone who does not take his cross and follow me is not worthy of me"— we suddenly find ourselves immersed in the promise of verse 39, where Jesus says, "Whoever finds his life will lose it, *and whoever loses his life for my sake will find it*" (italics mine). Speaking of comforting promises, by the way, just think of these blessed words that Jesus' followers have cherished for two millennia as recorded in Matthew 11:28: "Come to me, all you who are weary and burdened, and I will give you rest."

This blend of challenge and promise in Jesus' words is both striking and profound. One of the most gracious things about Jesus, I have always felt, is the way he simultaneously communicates both radical acceptance and a radical challenge to grow. He holds these seemingly opposite qualities in a marvelous creative tension, which

---

1. Payne, *The Healing Presence*, 167–71.

is surely why outcast and needy people flocked to him, while those who preferred to feel secure in themselves kept their distance.

Is it because I carry inside me qualities belonging to both these groups of people that I have always felt powerfully drawn to Jesus' radical acceptance even as I have also, at times, felt troubled by his radical challenges?

That is a disturbing thought. Yet surely God understands our conflicts and ambivalence. Divine mercy is infinite, and I cannot believe that the Lord presents us with an ultimatum when he invites us to embrace a more radical faith and trust. Rightly or wrongly, during my struggles over the years I have never felt that God was presenting me with a "now or never" or an "all or nothing" kind of choice. While I believe deeply that God longs for us to be able to tell him from the heart that we choose him, now and forever, over everything that the world and our natural human strengths have to offer, I also believe that God is infinitely patient. I believe that God will wait for us to reach this point, loving us with grace and mercy until we do. Moreover, each time that we yield to the Lord in the present conflict, the present crisis, even if we are motivated largely by personal need or desire, I cannot help believing that God will be right there with us, working in us through the Holy Spirit to ready us for the day when we are finally able to yield to him more deeply.

As we live prayerfully toward this day, meditating on God's loving acceptance and radical challenge, it can be very helpful to look at people we know personally whose lives exemplify solid commitment to the Lord, and to reflect on their stories. I do not mean that we should compare ourselves with them; I simply mean that we can take inspiration from the different ways we see God working in so many lives. So now I want to share with you how I have seen full surrender exemplified in the lives of two friends: Eartha and Judy.

STORIES OF SURRENDER: EARTHA AND JUDY

Eartha is a woman of deep faith whom I met a couple of decades ago when I jumped impulsively into the car one afternoon and headed an hour east over to Worcester to track her down, along with her husband Joe. I had read in the paper about their coffee house ministry to street people, a ministry that was uniting many city churches in a wonderful ecumenical spirit, and I had a great urge to get to know them. Talking with them that day was indeed exciting, and over the years Eartha and I have become dear friends, so that today she is one of the first people I go to when I have a question whose answer calls for spiritual maturity and discernment.

Eartha's growth into such deep faith did not come easily, though. Her journey with God began when she was a twenty-year-old single mother, raising her four-year-old son alone after her first husband left her. She was terrified of the future, especially terrified of winding up a poor Black woman on welfare with a bunch of kids. "My childhood had been so hard," she told me once as she was sharing her story with me over the phone, "that I had not trusted anyone but myself since I was eight years old. Money, power, and fame had become my idols." She worked hard to achieve them, too, going to college and getting a job in the business world as she was raising little Michael. In the eyes of everyone around her, Eartha excelled at all that she did. But on the inside, she was still living in fear.

"Now, around this time," she explained, "while I was seeking to know God by reading through the Bible, I sensed God calling me into a trust relationship. It was as if I could hear him whispering, 'Trust me,' to my heart. I actually yelled out loud, 'How can I trust a God I cannot see when I can't even trust my own mother whom I can see?' It seemed completely ridiculous to me that God would even ask that. Really, surrendering Lordship of my life was absolutely terrifying. That's why it was such a battle and took so long. I really did not think that letting go of the reins of my life was even a possibility.

"God continued to pursue me, though, demonstrating his love and faithfulness to me as I continued reading the Bible, seeking to know the Lord and to make sense out of my life. Throughout those three years, it felt like God was literally wooing me. His love confronted me everywhere I turned. It was weird, but in every love song randomly playing on the radio, I heard God pouring out his love to me. It felt like he was singing to me! The Lord was persistent in demonstrating his love in tangible and meaningful ways, reminding me that no one else would ever love me as much as he did. Jesus had already proved his love by dying on the cross to redeem me. He continually whispered to my heart, 'Trust me, trust me.'

"After I spent three years mentally wrestling with the implications of trusting God with my life, God finally won my heart. One evening I walked into the kitchen to get something from the refrigerator, but as I reached out to open it, the door appeared to be a big screen on which I watched my life flash before my eyes. As event after event unfolded before me, I was amazed by what I saw. In every situation I faced, the Lord had been there showing me what I should do. When I ignored the Lord's leading and did the things that *I* wanted to do, I was the one that got hurt. When I obeyed God's directions, things went well with me. This revelation shook me to my core. I was shaken by the reality that God loved me more than I loved myself. If I trusted him and did what he wanted me to do instead of what I wanted to do, my life would be better; things would work out better for me. It finally hit me that I could trust God, because it became crystal clear to me that day that God was on my side, not trying to harm me or control me. God was trying to protect me and help me. He only wanted my good. I realized that he valued my soul and loved me with all of my idiosyncrasies, sinfulness and flaws.

"Finally, I understood that surrender meant that I chose to relinquish the reins of my life, to trust a God I could not see, and willingly to allow him to be my Lord and Leader. I finally dared to believe what Jesus says in Matthew 10:39, 'Whoever finds his life will lose it, and whoever loses his life for my sake will find it.' Since then God's love for me has become the single greatest thing in my life, and nothing is more important to me. Money, power, and fame have paled in comparison."

Eartha's story was so powerful when she first shared it with me, that for a moment after she paused, I was silent. But I knew that I had one question, and finally I dared to ask it. Twice, I noticed, Eartha had spoken about relinquishing the reins of her life. For some reason, that little phrase flew out at me like a red flag. It almost sounded as if she were abandoning the right to make any of her own decisions or to take any responsibility for her life. Was I misunderstanding her here? I wanted to know.

"What you have to realize," Eartha told me, "is that surrendering to God didn't mean that I was losing my freedom of choice. God made us free moral agents and wants us to remain free moral agents. The Lord has never forced me to do anything. He always gives me a choice."

"So, for instance," I ventured, "when you got to the point that you abandoned your goals of money, power, and fame, you were doing that of your own free will, not because God forced you to do it. It was just that your love relationship with the Lord was getting so deep that the only choice you felt you could make, given the person you were becoming, was to turn away from goals that were the opposite of everything God stood for. Was that how it was?"

"Yes," she told me. "That was it. I was giving myself over in love to someone who loved me more than I loved myself. I was surrendering, yes; but I was surrendering into God's perfect love."

Surrendering into God's perfect love . . .

And now, besides Eartha, I also think of Judy . . .

I first introduced Judy early on in this book, speaking of her involvement in street ministry during the years she was raising four boys alone following divorce. I don't remember if she actually used the word "surrender" when she first told me her story, but that hardly matters; clearly, surrendering was what she did.

The pivotal moment came when a priest approached Judy to ask if she would consider resigning her nursing job and entering street ministry full time under the auspices of the diocese. His suggestion took her by surprise.

"Just imagine!" she exclaimed on the day she first told me her story. "The diocese offered me one thousand dollars to start up. One thousand dollars! And me with four sons to support! Oh, I was furious. I couldn't imagine I'd ever go through with it.

"Around this time, I was asked to speak about the ministry during a Good Friday service at a local church. Now, I remember all this very clearly. I was at home, standing in front of the mirror before that talk, combing my hair and having it out with God. I remember saying, 'God, this is going to be my swan song tonight. I've been ridiculous even to think about this. I'll do this talk tonight, okay, because I've promised to do that, but afterwards there won't be any more of this foolishness. I'm just going to continue with my nursing and maybe some of the street work on the side. I've got to be practical. I have my boys to support.'

"So, I went over to the church. Talked to the children and their parents, gave the children some little outfits from South America to wear, taught them to say their names, and 'hello' and 'good-bye,' in Spanish. I don't know whether I talked for two minutes or twenty minutes, and I have no idea what I said. But after it was over, they took up a collection.

"Well, they collected a kind of miracle amount. One child asked his mom why she had put so much money in the plate, and she said, 'I just really believed what that lady said.' But even as they were counting the donations afterwards, I remember saying to God: 'Okay, God, thanks—but no thanks. I don't care if every person in that that church donated three hundred dollars. I'm just not doing it.' Later, though, after the church was empty and the priest and everybody had gone home, I stayed there in front of the altar. Just sat there staring at this life-size, dark-skinned Body of Christ that looked down on me from over the altar. And still I was saying to him, 'I'm sorry, but this is just too foolish. I really just can't.'

"And then somehow—I don't know, maybe those kids had softened my heart in a way I hadn't realized—I seemed really to *see him* for the first time. And then when I saw him, suddenly without any idea that this was going to happen, I heard myself saying straight to Jesus, 'Well, you died for me. So, I guess I'm just going to have to die for you.' It happened in a moment . . . It just came out . . . Just like that. And you know, the strange thing is that I was so comfortable after that, like a huge burden had been lifted. It just felt like an enormous release. So, I knew it had to be the Holy Spirit.

"And there's one more thing I have to tell you about this experience, weird as it's going to sound, because the story wouldn't be fully honest without it." Judy had waited a moment and then, when she resumed speaking, her voice was hushed with awe. "Three years later, I happened to be talking with the pastor of that church, and I mentioned the Body of Christ I had seen over the altar that night.

Well, he didn't know what I was talking about! It turned out *there had never been a life-size Body of Christ in that church—not even a small one. Not even on that Good Friday.*"

Neither of us had spoken for a moment. Then at last, Judy had broken the silence.

"Well, within a week of my incredible conversation with Jesus after describing the ministry to those people at church, I had one more experience. I was on my hands and knees after supper one evening, sweeping up crumbs. I remember looking through the door from the dining room into the sitting room, and there were my boys in there watching TV. The thought flashed through my mind, 'What's going to become of us all?' And then suddenly, out of nowhere—and believe me, I am not one of these people who hear God speaking to them around every corner—I heard God's voice. He said, '*I will take care of you.*' Six words. Nothing more. And do you know, that center has always remained intact for me. Even if I'm taken away and tortured some day, I know now that God will keep that center intact."

Years later—just a few weeks ago as I type this, actually— I was talking with Judy again, before sharing her story here. I asked her how this had all affected her boys, and what they were doing now.

"Well" she told me, "it was a strange upbringing they had, no question about it. But in a way I guess it just seems normal to me now in retrospect. Anyway, as you know, all four of them turned out great. They're all very interested in other people, other cultures, very committed to humanitarian and ecological concerns and to standing up for justice in the different career paths they've chosen. But boy, did they have to learn to roll with the punches along the way!

"And yet really, you know, I think they always understood how much richer our lives were this way than they would have been otherwise. We've been paid off in aces, over the years. *Aces.* Not just with the letters and visits from all the people we've known, but with so much joy and love that comes with the experience. Why, once we got asked to an Arabic party, an Afro-American cookout, and a Hispanic fiesta and housewarming, all on one weekend! Just imagine! And we didn't even have to leave Attleboro!"

Looking back now on my first conversation with Judy, remembering how she radiated peace and joy, I find myself thinking again about something else she said to me that day about her relationship with Jesus. "One thing I've got to say," she had told me, "You better not start saying 'yes' to God unless you want your whole life to be turned upside down, because it's a very demanding love affair!"

A love affair . . . Yes, that's what it has been for Judy, just as it has been for Eartha. The Lord wooed Eartha with love songs and assurances that she could trust him, because he knew that was what she needed. The Lord wooed Judy by appearing to her above the altar that night as a dark-skinned life-size Body of Christ, reminding her how he had died for her. But also, of course, God had been wooing Judy during all those previous years as she was opening her heart and her home to the many neighbors she met along her path. And hadn't God wooed her most recently through those children who were listening to her words at the service? "Maybe those kids had softened my heart," Judy had said.

Wasn't that wooing her through neighbor love?

MORE REFLECTIONS ON SURRENDER

I am sharing these stories here as if I am revisiting them for the first time. But of course, that isn't true. I have visited and revisited these stories, the testimonies of these dear women, many times over the years, reflecting whenever I have done so on my own journey with God. This is a good thing, I think. Other people's experiences are important resources. As I said, it is not that we are meant to compare ourselves with them; still, we need the insights and inspiration they offer. Details from our friends' journeys flesh out a fuller picture of how God can work in our lives than we could ever get by musing on our own experiences alone.

Yet it is also true that our own stories are the ones over which ultimately, we need to pray, and about which we need to ask ourselves honest questions.

For a long time, I used to think my problem was simply that I feared losing control if I handed my life over to God, and of course that is part of what was going on. It cannot have been the whole answer, though; it doesn't make sense. After all, which of us truly has control over our lives? Tragedy can overwhelm us when we least expect it; loved ones can be lost to us in any manner of ways; a fatal illness can strike at any moment. And if we look beyond hypothetical threats in our immediate personal lives and focus on all the huge threats in the precarious wider world—cyber warfare, climate change, global pandemics, social upheaval—who can possibly think that we really control our circumstances? At best, the control we exercise is so very minimal and exists on the most limited of levels. To pretend otherwise is to cling to a massive illusion.

One day an obvious question occurred to me. What if it was *the illusion itself* that I had actually been trying to protect?

Elizabeth O'Connor writes about "our many selves" in a book of the same name. She explains that once, during a time of great stress, she had the sense that there were many different selves living within her, all voicing conflicting opinions and claims, none willing to attend to or consider the views of the others.[2] O'Connor is not speaking about clinical dissociation here. She is simply describing a phenomenon that many of us can probably recognize if we think back to times when we ourselves were caught between contradictory impulses and motivations that we experienced simultaneously.

Don't a lot of us have many selves? My own sudden insight that I had been trying to protect the *illusion* of having control over my life seemed so obvious that I could hardly believe I hadn't realized it before! What if my failure to acknowledge this much earlier had something to do with my *own* many selves?

I was brought up as a cherished and protected only child, and surely that little girl was living right there inside of me from childhood on, during all the experiences of loneliness, love, fear, hope, challenge, and breakthrough that I have been writing about in these pages. Yes, every one of these experiences was real and transformative in so many ways and on so many levels. And yes, I have been deeply privileged that so many other people have been willing to share their pain with me, deeply blessed to have sensed Jesus'

2. O'Connor, *Our Many Selves*, 3.

presence with us all at the center of that pain, drawing us closer to one another and closer to him.

Yet even as I was praying for these neighbors and we were living through so many experiences together in Jesus' presence, wasn't that little girl still hiding away somewhere deep inside of me, clinging to the illusory comfort of pretending that her small protected world was what truly mattered? At times she must have been shutting her eyes tight and shaking her head hard, not wanting to look very honestly or for very long at everything God might want to show her, or at all the places God might want to lead her, if she truly surrendered to him ... Just as she once froze and found herself unable to follow when Jesus held out his hand during the wee hours of the morning while he stood in that wide, dark field, littered with those broken bodies, in my dream vision so many decades ago.

"The heart is deceitful above all things," we read in Scripture (Jeremiah 17:9).

Eventually the day came when I realized that if I were ever going to be able to surrender more deeply to God, I would have to do one crucial thing first.

I would have to ask the Lord to change my heart.

ASKING GOD TO CHANGE OUR HEARTS

And now I have one last story to share with you. Once again, this story springs from a relationship that began in neighbor-love, though it grew far beyond that. By now, of course, this neighbor-love connection should be no surprise, for I really do believe that in the command to love our neighbors as ourselves, God has given us a kind of operational definition of one possible pathway into intimacy with the Lord. There is something about the journey into neighbor-love that really does open our hearts to God. So now, this final story begins with the day that I met Jean.

Jean is a dear woman whom I got to know many years ago at The Refuge, the home-based retreat ministry of my friend Faith. Jean's therapist had suggested that she spend a weekend there to try to work through some issues she was dealing with; and as it happened,

I was visiting at the same time. So, there we were—spontaneous and providential neighbors! We had lunch together in Faith's lovely dining room and later, as Jean and I were out raking leaves in the back yard, Jean revealed to me that she was grappling with post-traumatic stress disorder in the wake of memories that had recently been surfacing regarding abusive childhood experiences.

That weekend at Faith's house was the beginning of an unfolding friendship between Jean and me, a friendship that has deepened over the years as I have come to see Jean's integrity and the enormous courage with which she has faced inner challenges I can scarcely imagine. Beyond this, Jean is a deeply gifted woman whose generous heart prompts her to reach out to many folks in need. (I introduced her briefly in an earlier chapter, actually, describing her extraordinary conversation with a perfect stranger, during which that stranger was moved to healing tears.) In my own life, as well, I cannot begin to count the times that Jean has been there for me when I have needed her. Sometimes the crisis in question was worthy of a TV sit-com that I was too embarrassed to share with anyone else—like the time I once fell asleep in the bathtub, numb with exhaustion while the faucets were still on, waking up later to find that the overflowing water had soaked through the floor and turned the basement below into a kind of mini fresh water ocean, on the surface of which was floating an inflated rubber globe! It was Jean, of course, whom I asked to come help me dry out and clean up. She has never let me forget that globe, by the way, and still reminds me of it occasionally in moments of light-hearted reminiscence. But I digress . . .

In any event, it was as we were driving back together from a couple of days on Cape Cod many years after we first met, and just before the stressful decade when I was immersed in caring for my elderly parents, that Jean and I shared the experience which proved to be such a turning point for me in my own relationship with God. We had been working at a small rental cottage I owned at the time, readying it for the season's first tenant. It was getting dark as we sped along the turnpike back to western Massachusetts, but in the dim light of the car, I could pick up the tension on Jean's face and in her voice. "How is it?" I asked, meaning the pain which I knew had been gathering in her leg over the past hour. "Memory pain," the doctor called it; it signaled an imminent flashback to some as yet unsurfaced memory.

Jean didn't answer for a moment, but she didn't need to. I knew she was in bad shape. "What can I do, Lord?" I prayed silently. "I can't handle this. What if a memory surfaces for her here while I'm driving? What if she goes into a coma or has a stroke? What can I do? I can't handle this." But of course, this was one of those times when to say "I can't" was irrelevant, for the simple fact was that I had to. I had no other choice.

I put my right hand on Jean's leg, steering with my left, and silently began to pray. "Jesus, you know how I fear abandoned surrender to you, how feeble my own faith often is. I'm not a prayer warrior like Faith, and I have so many unanswered questions. But oh, Lord, here we are, and I'm the only one here. Lord, please help her. *Help us*. Please touch Jean in her pain."

We drove on in silence for a few moments. Then, very quietly, Jean spoke. "Were you praying for me back then?" she wanted to know.

"Yes, I was," I told her. "Why do you ask?"

"I wondered," she said, "because I felt a flash of heat going through my leg when you had your hand on it."

"*Oh*," I breathed. And my eyes filled with tears.

I knew Jean shouldn't be alone that night. Her husband Kenny wouldn't be available; he was working a night shift. But strangely, given the depth of that prayer experience in the car, as I sat at Jean's bedside through the long night, encouraging her to talk to me, to help me stay in touch with what was happening to her, I found myself seriously blocked when it came to discerning how God wanted me to pray. Surely, I should be praying that Jean could trust God more deeply and open herself to his healing power as she fought for control and battled the onslaught of memories. But the right words were not coming to me; I could sense that something was blocking me in my spirit.

How can we pray with power that another person be open to a gift which we ourselves are resisting? Because wasn't I still struggling with issues of trust and control in my own relationship with God?

One morning in the wake of that insight, I found myself scribbling a few lines in my journal. Their precision and their stark honesty stunned me. Here is what I wrote. "To make a full surrender to God *with my will*, from a place of felt strength, I must first ask God to change my heart and ready me for it. How might he do that? Unpredictable. That's the risk—for the pearl of great price."

It was the first time I had actually recognized and articulated to myself that I needed to ask God to change my heart.

A few weeks later, a drear drizzly sky hung over the landscape as I headed alone to Cape Cod on another quick business trip. I had to tend to some more errands at my little rental cottage before the next tenant's arrival. Once I got there, I quickly completed those real estate duties. Several hours stretched ahead before it turned dark, and I decided to go for a walk. I took a couple of books with me— the Bible and an anthology of Kierkegaard that we were reading for a book group to which I belonged—and headed for the beach.

The rain had stopped by then, though it was still damp and gray. People had begun to gather in little clumps, strolling along the road— some in casual beach wear, others dressed for dinner at one of the waterside restaurants. Everywhere I looked, it seemed, I saw families: husbands, wives, children. Normally this didn't make me feel lonely, but on this particular afternoon it did. I found a spot between two rocks, nestled down, and opened my Bible. "Anyone who loves his father or mother more than me is not worthy of me; anyone who loves his son or daughter more than me is not worthy of me," I read in Matthew 10:37. Families again. Jesus' words calling his disciples to a higher love than the strictly human served only to remind me, as I huddled there between those rocks, how bereft of family my divorce had left me feeling in my own life. At that moment, for some reason, none of the experiences of neighbor-love which generally seemed so meaningful brought their usual comfort.

Closing the Bible and picking up Kierkegaard, I turned to one of the selections assigned for our book group's next meeting. The content of that particular passage, though, only intensified the weight of isolation pressing down on me. Kierkegaard's brooding reflections there on the existential demands of faith, the naked relationship between the Christian and his or her God, unrelieved by the comfort of communal caring, were more than I could bear. I had always understood that the horror of human isolation lay at the root of my calling into neighbor-love. Now, though, even that call felt abstract and remote. All I felt was loneliness.

I thought back to the days so long ago when my marriage was breaking up, remembering the ecstatic wonder of feeling Jesus' presence and love palpably surrounding me, comforting me, and reassuring me through all my senses that he would never leave me. Yet just a year or so later, I was choosing—yes, choosing—to take autonomous steps into single again living, consciously thinking as I did so, "God, I know you want me to trust you entirely and to promise always to seek your will rather than my own. But Lord, at this point I just don't know how to do that. It feels to me like a life or death necessity to develop my autonomous strength right now in the wake of this failed marriage." The implication seemed clear—even if it meant sacrificing intimacy with him.

Once, I remembered, a Catholic sister whose storefront drop-in center I had briefly frequented during separation was conducting a series of teachings on the gospel of John. Knowing that she planned to celebrate a Eucharistic meal with us on the day she taught John 6, I had deliberately stayed away. I knew, given her style, that as she broke bread among us and spoke of Jesus' broken body, she would invite us all to give ourselves to be broken as well—broken for Jesus, broken with him for the world. And I knew that I couldn't make that commitment. To the depths of my soul, I felt that what I needed most was to develop some personal strength of my own.

Only now, on this gray afternoon so many years later, it felt as though all the natural resources I had been building and cherishing were turning to ashes around me. What were they really worth, after all? In the abstract I had long understood that phrase "false securities," but never had I experienced its meaning quite as palpably as I did that afternoon. Would my little house protect me against the inevitability of eventual sickness and death? Would my bank account save me from my own mortality? It was God's presence, God's love, God's peace, that I would need on the day that my natural strength failed me. All my worldly symbols of security and even joy—my little cottage that I loved with all my heart, for example—in this moment bespoke nothing but loneliness, isolation, and pain.

I heard myself whisper aloud, *"Jesus, please don't leave me,"* as tears filled my eyes and streamed down my cheeks.

I went to bed early that night. I didn't even make the bed, just threw my sleeping bag over the bedspread, and sprawled out on it in my clothes, falling into a fitful sleep.

Did I dream? Not that I remember. Yet when I awoke the next morning, even as I was first opening my eyes, I could sense that on a deep level—deep, deep down—something profound had taken place. Something in my heart had been healed.

Raising myself up on one elbow, I looked out the window at the pure blue sky, the gnarled branches of scrub pine that I so loved and that had always spelled "Cape Cod" to me. The breeze stirring through the open window ruffled the soft white curtains and touched my cheek. Oh, the serenity of that moment, the breathtaking joy of this new day!

I went out to the kitchen, made coffee, and walked with my mug the half mile down to the beach. On every side an invisible chorus of silent angels seemed to be singing for joy, offering praise and thanks and glory. My heart joined in that silent chorus. *"Thank you, Jesus, thank you, thank you."*

Back at my cottage again, as I sat there on the deck, one thought washed over my soul: the mercy, the never-ending mercy of the Lord.

How despairing I had been just eight short hours ago. Yet now, what joy flooded my heart!

Surely Christ had been holding me fast all these years, despite my own weakness and fear— in speaking to me about the importance of neighbor- love for my own journey . . . in guiding me into healing, transforming relationships with men and women in our shelter . . . in introducing me to Jean as a new neighbor, bringing me into friendship with her, and gracing me so recently to write those crucial words in my journal after I felt blocked in my spirit while trying to pray for her. I picked up the journal and reread that entry.

"To make a full surrender to God *with my will*, from a place of felt strength, I must first ask God to change my heart and ready me for it. How might he do that? Unpredictable. That's the risk—for the pearl of great price."

Yes, that was it. Only during my experience, the evening before, I had certainly not been in "a place of felt strength"!

A Bible lay on the deck chair beside me. Turning to the passage I had deliberately avoided confronting in Sister Joyce's class so many years ago, this is what I read: "I tell you the truth, you are looking for me . . . because you ate the loaves and had your fill. Do not work for food that spoils, but for food that endures to eternal life, which the Son of Man will give you" (John 6:26–27).

My eyes filled with tears. Jesus might have been right there with me, speaking those words.

I picked up my journal, my pen, and began to write. And as the words poured out on the page, I realized I was writing a prayer:

> Lord, thank you for the experience of peace and joy here in solitude reflecting on you, in contrast to yesterday's lonely despair. Thank you for speaking to us through your Word, and for sending me to John 6. I do ask you now to change my heart so I will finally be able to give myself to you completely.
>
> I ask this knowing I cannot predict what you will do or the means you will use to change my heart—that it even could involve losing this beautiful place I so love. But I am content to risk that because I really do begin to understand at last that apart from my relationship with you, all earthly beauty ultimately turns to ashes anyway. So, I ask this—that you will change my heart and draw me closer to you— in full awareness of the implications that have for so many years seemed so frightening, but that now, for whatever reason, somehow don't feel so frightening anymore . . .Yes Lord, please change my heart.

There on the deck, in the sun, I read it over.

Had I written that? Did I mean it?

I read it again: one, twice, a third time.

Yes, the substance held. I had written it. I did mean it.

And then I knew something else: that now, at last, this journey had truly begun.

REFLECTIVE QUESTIONS: CHAPTER 6

1. What connotations does the word "surrender" hold for you? If a healthy autonomy is desirable at times, humanly speaking, is there any place for autonomy in one's relationship with God? Why or why not? What are the differences?

2. Who in your life most clearly embodies for you a radical surrender to God? What qualities in this person's style of faith inspire you? What qualities disturb or frighten you? Why?

3. When you are feeling most needy and broken are you able to abandon yourself to God's grace and guidance, or do you usually feel a need to "get it together" under your own strength first? When you are feeling strong and all is going well, how ready are you to become broken again, if God should ask that of you?

4. In a general sense, do you feel able to believe with your heart as well as with your mind Jesus' promise in Matthew 10:39 that "whoever loses his life for my sake will find it"?

5. Which of Jesus' promises feel to you most gracious and reassuring? Which of his commands or challenges frighten you most deeply? Try to hold some promises and challenges in your mind and heart at the same time, so that it is no longer a matter of "either/or" but rather a matter of "both/and." How does this feel? As an example, consider these two verses: "Come to me, all you who are weary and burdened, and I will give you rest" (Matthew 11:28); and "anyone who does not take his cross and follow me is not worthy of me" (Matthew 10:38).

Concluding Word

As I shared in the Preface, recently I resumed work on this manuscript after a hiatus of twenty-some years during which I was immersed in parent care and my second marriage. Picking up where I had left off and beginning to rework what I had previously written, I decided not to include in the narrative new personal material drawn from those intervening years. That prospect felt too overwhelming. Instead, I want to share a few stories and reflections here, in this Concluding Word, and to link them up with themes that I have been exploring throughout these pages.

Anyone who has been intensively involved in caring for aged parents surely knows the challenges that come with the task. But there can be huge blessings as well, particularly when God gives us opportunities to heal old hurts and wounds. As a much loved and highly protected only child, I need to confess that in my protracted efforts to struggle toward a sense of independent strength during young adulthood, I know that I hurt my parents badly—especially Mother. It was a great gift when those years of caring for her during her battle with cancer gave me the chance to practice loving her with something closer to agape love than I had been capable of showing her before.

I remember one experience in particular. Mother was lingering in the hospital at one point after surgery that had gone badly wrong, and her surgeon asked if I could think of anything she might be willing to eat. On a sudden impulse I brought her a thermos of tomato soup, together with a small porcelain cup out of which she used to give *me* tomato soup when I was sick as a child. She remembered! I held it out to her, and smiling through her tears, she drank it and then asked for more. As I shared in a devotional that I once wrote about this experience, in that moment it seemed as though in some miraculous and gracious way God perfectly healed those painful memories of Mother's and my struggles over the years.[1]

After Mother's death the blessings continued, especially after I brought Daddy up to a nursing home in Northampton a few minutes from my house, where he had a private room which I fixed up like a tiny studio apartment, complete with a microwave and a mini-fridge. I visited him several times daily as my work schedule permitted and (unbeknownst to him!) paid several friends to spend time with him as well, so that he was rarely alone. He especially loved my dear friend Andrea, whose lilting warmth and charm completely captivated him. One day she came flying through the door of my kitchen (at that time she lived in the little apartment I had built above my ranch house), calling out to me, "Your daddy accepted Jesus today! Your daddy accepted Jesus!"

Indeed, he had, as became movingly evident in the months that followed. He wept over a beautiful tape I played him containing a talk on grace by Philip Yancey; he listened with tears in his eyes during Sunday afternoon services in the home's activity room; and talking about the Lord's Prayer, he told me one day that he tried to make it more personal for himself by asking God to make him a better father to me. Just think of it—all this coming from a man who had been a life-long agnostic till the age of ninety-four!

The most blessed time, though, came one afternoon as he was lying in his recliner while I perched on the end of his bed. Talking about our relationship over the years, he confessed that although he had come to appreciate me so much more during the years I had been caring for Mother and him, there was still one thing he could not forgive. He could not forgive me for having hurt Mother so badly during those years in the past.

Looking into his eyes, I told him gently, "Daddy, you know that she forgave me years ago for all that. And I honestly think that

1. Chase, "A White Porcelain Cup," 233–35.

if you could find it in your heart to forgive me as well, you would feel so very, very much better."

He looked at me for a long moment. Then, finally, he raised his right arm as if delivering a benediction and very slowly, with utter seriousness, he pronounced eight words. "I forgive you," he said. "I see it no more."

A few months later, he died.

And then, a few years after that, I married Chip.

What shall I tell you here about Chip's and my decade together? I already mentioned in the Preface that during the first two years of our marriage, before his retirement and our move back to my house in Northampton, I had the privilege of sharing his pastoral ministry with him, and I continue to regard this experience as one of the most precious gifts in my life. We also had challenges, though, especially after he retired, for we had utterly different temperaments, and we came to remarriage later in life after decades of single-again living following our respective divorces. Nonetheless, with mutual prayer, commitment, and effort, we continued to grow into deeper harmony. During the last few years of our marriage Chip would sometimes whisper, almost in awe, "We're so blessed. God has given us such a wonderful life." Tears of thankfulness fill my eyes even now as I write this.

Gratitude for God's grace in our marriage and the ways he helped us grow to love each other more deeply in the midst of our respective flaws came to me most profoundly, perhaps, in September of 2020 as I was reliving memories of our last year together, about nine months after Chip's unexpected passing in December of 2019. Sitting at the living room table in our little Cape Ann condo which he so loved, I was rereading my 2019 journal when amazingly, I had the most extraordinary sense that both God and Chip were right there in the room *with* me, blessing our marriage. A couple of hours later as I was walking by the sea, listening on my phone to a sermon by Greg Boyd, one of the preachers I follow online, Boyd's image suddenly disappeared from the screen, and in its place up popped a photo of Chip praying with three other men. This was a picture I had taken at College Church way back in 2015, five years earlier, on an old flip phone I had long since lost, together with all the pictures in its gallery! I feel hesitant to presume a miracle here; perhaps there is some physical explanation for this technological marvel that is simply beyond my ken. Whatever the cause, this amazing event felt to me like a providential "seal" on the blessing I had experienced God and Chip giving to our marriage earlier that afternoon. When I told my friend Eartha about this, she smiled. "Yes," she said. "I know those experiences. I call them 'little kisses.'"

The blessings our marriage brought into my life still continue, by the way, as I grow into deeper relationships these days with Chip's fantastic son Charles (or "Colin," as Chip called him, using his childhood nickname) and Chip's lovely daughter Abigail. I have "grandchildren" now, too; Colin and Abby each have their own respective families—four wonderful children between the two of them. While Abby lives far from Northampton, way over in western Pennsylvania, Colin lives just a half hour away from my house, and babysitting beautiful little Jackie every Wednesday afternoon, being "Grandma Tibby" to her as I watch her grow by leaps and bounds, is bringing new joy into my life these days.

How many personal memories I have been sharing in this Concluding Word! One might ask whether these really belong at the end of a book that, up until now, has been about neighbor-love. Actually, I believe that they do. I remember suggesting earlier that the way our relationships with neighbors can gradually transform our hearts may have something in common with the growth that occurs in healthy families when, over time, we develop more mature ways of caring and learn to let go of egocentric patterns. The obvious difference, of course, is that with neighbor-love we have no prior personal relationship on which to build; we simply start at the outset by offering intentional agape love, and let God take it from there.

The implications here are very rich. What if it can also work the other way around? Speaking for myself, I know that sometimes when I have been anguished or angered in my personal relationships, I have attempted to detach from expectations I carry about how my loved one "should" be treating me (as my mother, father, husband, good friend, or whatever) and have tried instead (though often not very successfully!) to treat that loved one as if he or she were, for the moment, simply my neighbor, whom God is calling me to love.

To give ourselves over to this process can sometimes involve real surrender, of course—the surrender of deep personal longing in order to accept and enter more creatively into whatever the present reality actually offers. Perhaps not surprisingly, as I mention the word "surrender" while writing this now, I find myself thinking about that experience I shared at the end of the last chapter, when I asked God to change my heart to help me surrender more fully to him. Has God been answering that prayer?

Yes, I believe that God has—though perhaps not in exactly the way I was envisioning those many years ago. Just as conversion can happen gradually for some people, rather than through one dramatic and identifiable "born again" experience, I wonder if something analogous cannot occur when it comes to the process of surrender. I cannot point back over the years to one dramatic and identifiable moment when I permanently and completely surrendered to the Lord once and for all; nor (which is equally significant) do I remember a time when I felt God was asking me to surrender then and there in that fashion and I refused to do so. Yet a little over a year ago, shortly after Chip's death, I had a very moving experience. The reason why I do not identify this as an initial once-and-for-all moment of surrender will become clear as I describe what happened.

Once again, I was listening on YouTube to a sermon by Greg Boyd, this time a sermon that he had originally preached back on July 6, 2014, entitled "Twisted Scripture: Romans 10." At the very end of this sermon, Boyd projected onto the screen a "Prayer of Surrender." He stressed that surrendering our lives to the Lord means that we enter a covenantal relationship, much like marriage, and he invited anyone who felt so led to read the words of that prayer aloud with him, then and there— either as a first-time pledge or as reaffirmation of a promise previously given.[2]

Suddenly all military implications of the word "surrender" that had disturbed me so much for so long completely fell away,

---

2. Boyd, "Twisted Scripture."

and in their place, I sensed only the rich and beautiful associations belonging to the marriage covenant. When we marry, after all, even while we vow to love and to cherish as long as we live, implicitly we realize there are bound to be times in the future when we will fall short of this ideal, times when we will need God's forgiveness and grace to encourage us to move forward. Somehow, to think of surrender in the context of this marriage metaphor made all the difference.

At that moment I felt in my heart that I could honestly speak the words of that prayer; and so I did. As I heard myself promising to seek and to follow the Lord's will from that moment on, to yield my life to him, always relying on his grace to support, encourage, and forgive me when I failed, I had a strange feeling that this was not the first time I had committed myself to God in this fashion; somehow, in a way that I cannot explain, I sensed in my spirit that I was indeed reaffirming a commitment I had already made and had even, perhaps, already reaffirmed one or more times in the past—consciously or subconsciously, wordlessly or with other words entirely, that now I could not even remember. That I could not identify the exact moment(s) nor recall the exact words somehow did not seem to matter. Something had taken place—something *was* taking place—beyond my capacity to analyze or understand.

Isn't it all mystery, Lord? How can we understand it—how can we understand anything—apart from you?

If we look beyond the stories I have been sharing in these pages to everything looming over us in the wider world,—pandemics, injustice, social upheaval, climate change, polarization, cyber warfare, starvation, violence, and so many defying your standards in so many ways—how can we dare really to face it and feel the pain of it all, unless we trust that you are truly with us in the midst of it? Yet if we look honestly, Lord, we do see that you are with us, in so many acts of mercy and lives of love all around us, as well as in our own hearts.

Help us, dear God, to see it all through the lens of your infinite love, sovereign and vulnerable at the same time, as you pour yourself out for us even now just as once, Lord Jesus, you poured yourself out for us on the cross. Give each of us faith to live as you call us to live, in the spirit of Romans 8:28, trusting that you will redeem us and bring good out of this chaos for the sake of your ultimate kingdom, in ways we cannot fathom or foresee. And please, Lord, as we live into this mystery through the power of your Holy Spirit, give us the grace to surrender to you more completely: to love you with all of our heart, soul, strength, and mind, and to love our neighbors as ourselves. Amen.

Bibliography

Barton, Ruth Haley. *Sacred Rhythms: Arranging Our Lives for Spiritual Transformation*. Downers Grove: IVP, 2006.

Berlin, Tom. *Reckless Love: Jesus' Call to Love Our Neighbor*. Nashville: Abingdon, 2019.

Boyd, Greg. "Twisted Scripture: Romans 10." July 6, 2014. https://whchurch. org/sermon/ twisted-scripture-romans-10.

Burt, Alan R. *Blessings of the Burden: Reflections and Lessons in Helping the Homeless*. Grand Rapids: Eerdmans, 2013.

Chase, Elise. "A White Porcelain Cup." In *My Turn to Care: Affirmations for Caregivers of Aging Parents*, compiled and edited by Marlene Bagnull, 233–35. Nashville: Thomas Nelson, 1994.

Labberton, Mark. *The Dangerous Act of Loving Your Neighbor: Seeing Others Through the Eyes of Jesus*. Downers Grove: IVP, 2010.

Lewis, C. S. *The Four Loves*. New York: Harcourt, Brace, 1960.

———. *Mere Christianity: A revised and amplified edition, with a new introduction, of the three books Broadcast Talks, Christian Behaviour and Beyond Personality*. New York: HarperOne, 2001.

Linnell, Patrick. *Grace Bomb: The Surprising Impact of Loving Your Neighbors*. Colorado Springs: David C. Cook, 2021

Nouwen, Henri J. M. *The Road to Daybreak: A Spiritual Journey*. New York: Image, 1990.

Nouwen, Henri J. M., with Michael J. Christensen and Rebecca J. Laird. *Spiritual Formation: Following the Movements of the Spirit*. New York: HarperOne, 2015.

O'Connor, Elizabeth. *Call to Commitment*. New York: Harper & Row, 1963.

———. *Journey Inward, Journey Outward*. New York: Harper & Row, 1968.

———. *Our Many Selves*. New York: Harper & Row, 1971.

Payne, Leanne. *The Healing Presence: How God's Grace Can Work in You to Bring Healing in Your Broken Places and the Joy of Living in His Love*. Westchester: Crossway, 1989.

BIBLIOGRAPHY

Tozer, A. W. *The Knowledge of the Holy: The Attributes of God: Their Meaning in the Christian Life*. New York: HarperSanFrancisco, 1961.

Woofenden, Anna, and Derrick Weston, co-hosts. "Friends at the Table: A Conversation with Lee Anderson," May 24, 2021. www.foodandfaith.org.

Yancey, Philip. *What's So Amazing about Grace?* Grand Rapids: Zondervan, 1997.